10
Secrets
to Building
a Winning
Business

ALSO BY ANDREW GRIFFITHS

101 Ways to Market Your Business
101 Ways to Advertise Your Business
101 Ways to Really Satisfy Your Customers
101 Ways to Boost Your Business
101 Ways to Have a Business and a Life
101 Ways to Build a Successful Network Marketing Business

101

Secrets
to Building
a Winning
Business

Andrew Griffiths

ALLEN&UNWIN

First published under the title *Secrets to Building a Winning Business* in 2005
This revised edition published in 2008

Allen & Unwin
83 Alexander Street
Crows Nest NSW 2065
Australia
Phone: (61 2) 8425 0100
Fax: (61 2) 9906 2218
Email: info@allenandunwin.com
Web: www.allenandunwin.com

National Library of Australia
Cataloguing-in-Publication entry:

Griffiths, Andrew, 1966-

101 secrets to building a winning business

ISBN 978 1 74175 567 1 (pbk.)

Bibliography.

Success in business—Handbooks, manuals, etc.
Business planning—Handbooks, manuals, etc.

650.1

Set in 12/14 pt Adobe Garamond by Midland Typesetters, Australia
Printed and bound in Australia by Griffin Press

10 9 8 7 6 5 4 3 2 1

Contents

Acknowledgments

This book is now the seventh title in the *101 Ways* series. A huge milestone for me and, I am sure, for my publishers, who for some strange reason keep asking me to write more books. I don't think any of us realised just how big and bold this series would become. Today these books are sold around the world. As an Australian it is very rewarding to be accepted as an international authority on the subject of small business. As a result I get to spread my passionate messages about the importance of small business in every country and, most importantly of all, I get to help people build the business of their dreams. This makes every long night spent at my computer worthwhile. So I would like to dedicate this book to those exceptional entrepreneurs who have gladly shared their stories with me, their incredible journeys and their love for what they do. Thank you for helping me to do what I do.

On a more indulgent note, I would also like to thank my new brother, Sen Ekanayake, for the most amazing support a friend has ever given me; Robert Reid, my literary confidant and all-round good mate; John MacKenzie, the ex-Gladstone postie and rock-solid supporter; and of course, Dr Debra Lawson, the cherry on my cake.

'The greatest revolution of our generation
is the discovery that human beings,
by changing the inner attitudes of their minds,
can change the outer aspects of their lives.'
William James, Harvard psychologist

Introduction

Some people seem to be born with the entrepreneurial gene. From the earliest of ages they are driven to set up businesses that sell anything and everything from lemonade on the side of the road to kittens. I completely understand this compulsion as my first business was selling newspapers to local businesses in Perth at around the age of 7 or 8. Since then I have pretty well been in business in some shape or form, doing everything from commercial diving, selling encyclopaedias door to door, advertising, travel, tourism and others that I have simply forgotten or tried to forget.

I couldn't imagine not running my own business. I love the challenge, I love being my own boss and I love the feeling of having control of my destiny (or at least feeling like I have).

We all have to deal with increased competition, in fact I think this is a good thing. Although there are lots of new businesses starting every day, most are not that good at what they do. So if you are better than the rest, you can't help but succeed and that is exactly what *101 Secrets to Building a Winning Business* will help you to achieve.

Today I get to share my experience and knowledge with literally thousands of people, through my books and seminars. I have been working with small business owners around the world for many years. I am constantly amazed by their innovation, their energy and their commitment. It is truly spectacular.

That said, I encounter a lot of businesses that really struggle and I have been in the same place myself many times.

In my opinion there are two types of businesses; those that have had hard times and those that are going to have hard times. It's really difficult when times are tough and the biggest irony is that most of the issues could generally have been avoided if the business owner had been given good advice in the first place.

So, I want to share what I have learnt through my own experiences and through the experiences I have observed or had passed on from some exceptionally successful business-people around the world. In the following pages there are 121 tips that will certainly increase your chances of business success.

In *101 Secrets to Building a Winning Business* I put a very significant focus on actioning the recommendations I put forward. Sit back, grab a pen and get cracking on what I hope will be a very interesting and exciting journey in your entrepreneurial life.

What is the difference between success and failure?

I get asked this question a lot and it is not an easy one to answer. Sure we can look at a bank account balance but if that was the only indicator we had to measure an entrepreneur's success it would be a sad world indeed. Personally, I believe anyone who is brave enough to step out of their comfort zone and enter the challenging world of self-employment should already be classified as a significant success because there is no doubt that running your own business is tough. However, I have noticed that most financially successful entrepreneurs share common personality characteristics and an overriding desire to be good at what they do. I cover these characteristics throughout this book and you may be surprised to notice how many you have. Often this is what drives people to be entrepreneurs in the first place—they are good at what they do and they know it and they would rather make money for themselves than someone else.

If I had to pick one defining characteristic that separates success and failure it would have to be passion. Those entrepreneurs who are passionate about their businesses will not accept half measures—they sincerely want to be the best at what they do. They are passionate regarding their products and services, their customers and their staff. This passion enables them to embrace change and face the everyday challenges that all business owners face head-on. Sure they encounter set backs but they don't get caught up in the negatives, preferring instead to move forward, learning from their mistakes and refining the way they do things. They are passionate enough to share their triumphs and tragedies in a philosophical way and they will help other people to succeed wherever they can.

Size doesn't matter

One of my greatest frustrations is what I call the 'Small Business Syndrome' and I refer to it often in my books. This is where the eternal excuse for not being able to run a business to its full potential is the fact that it is 'only a small business'. From my own experiences the best run businesses are small businesses and size is certainly no excuse for not providing great service, doing smart marketing, making great products or being innovative and dynamic. Often small business owners are almost apologetic for being a small business. I think it is well and truly time to move on from this mindset and embrace the fact that small businesses are the engine of the business world—there are millions of them and they generally lead the way in all industries.

Being small is no excuse—it is a wonderful opportunity. Imagine being the CEO of a huge multinational corporation— how do you make a change to the way the business operates? There needs to be countless meetings, often leading to arguments for change, board approval, then the changes need to be handed down to the next level to start the long and winding road to implementation. Once this road is navigated the changes eventually reach the front-counter staff who actually sell the product or service. In a small business if you want to make a change—you just do it. How empowering is that?

My main message here is to be proud of your business, regardless of the size. Building a winning business has nothing to do with size—it is all about attitude.

Do you have the commitment to build a successful business?

As an author I meet a lot of people who want to write a book. In fact I am amazed at how many people have this dream. But of all the people who want to write a book very few actually do it. The real question here is why not? Coming up with a good idea for a book is pretty easy. I'm sure most of us could sit down with a pen and paper and come up with a few good ideas in a couple of minutes. But what happens once these great ideas are staring back at us from a sheet of paper?

Writing a book takes time, commitment and discipline—just like running a successful business. When I got the phone call from my publishers saying they liked the manuscript for my first book enough to publish it I assumed I could put my feet up, sit back, go to eBay and buy my first Porsche. The reality was a little different. My publishers did like the idea but I had to rewrite the entire manuscript from start to finish. They edited it three times and it took almost twelve months before it was ready to hit the printers. Finally, the book was ready to go on the shelves and this was where the real nitty gritty of selling stepped in.

Running a successful business is a lot like writing and publishing a book. It's very easy to fall in love with the idea but the reality is that it will take a lot of time, dedication, discipline and hard work just to get it up and running, and then there is no guarantee it will work. Successful business entrepreneurs have this commitment and dedication and, from my observations, this is a characteristic of their personality type. It is not something they have to decide to do—it just happens.

My advice here is simple: if you're not 100 per cent committed to building a very successful business . . . get a job. Enjoy a weekly pay cheque (there is nothing wrong with that) but don't fall in love with the romantic concept of owning your own business or it will end in tears and heartache.

The best way to use this book

We all read 'how to' books in our own way. Some people like to start at the beginning and work their way through to the end, point by point. Others prefer to open up at any page and take note of the tip that presents itself, while some others prefer to use the contents page to guide them to the most relevant passages in the book. It really is up to you. But the most important piece of advice I would give you is to make sure you keep an open mind to all of the tips and recommendations made in this book. Think about applying them to your business and visualise the end result of making the change. This is the kind of book that needs to be read and re-read. I believe that often the most pressing issues seem to stand out on the page and it is easy to overlook other recommendations. But if you put the book down and pick it up again in six months, the issues that were relevant during your first reading have changed and all of a sudden the current issues are the ones standing out.

Recurring themes

Throughout this book you will come across a number of themes that are repeated and emphasised. There is good reason for this: they are very important points. For those people who like to flick from section to section, they will not miss these key points and recurring themes. For those who read a book cover to cover, I don't mean to nag, I am just reinforcing the key issues for making a mediocre business magnificent. Some of these key points include the importance of building strong relationships, the need to be able to promote yourself and your business unashamedly, the need to have good advisers and the need to think like a successful entrepreneur from day one.

Some themes are very tangible, some are more philosophical, but both are equally important. Business success is as much in our heads as it is with the products and services we sell.

Without action it's all a waste of time

I write lots of marketing plans for companies all over the world. They can be detailed plans for large corporations or simpler plans for small business owners. The thickness of the plan is normally proportional to the size of the business and, regardless of this, they look very impressive sitting on the shelf. But if that is where they stay, they are useless.

I love going into a client's business and watching them pull out a marketing plan I prepared and it is covered in pen marks, coffee stains, occasionally lipstick (which always has me a little intrigued) and various other signs of human contact. This means the marketing plan is being used—it is being read and re-read. They are questioning my recommendations—reviewing what to do and when to do it. Likewise the recommendations in this book, in fact in all of my books, need to be actioned. They are crying out for it. I try to make sure I explain how to implement the ideas in a simple, no-nonsense manner.

To encourage and help you action the recommendations I am suggesting I have included an immediate 'Things to do now' section at the end of each tip. This is what you can do today to get your business on track to becoming as successful as you want it to be. Write all over the pages. There is also an action list at the end of each chapter. There is a brainstorming page at the end of each section—write on it, anything that comes to mind.

If you action one point every day for the next 120 days imagine how much closer your business will be to reaching its full potential—an exciting thought. If one per day is too ambitious try one per week—the results will be the same, but they will take longer to achieve. So it is up to you. Remember to delegate if you can (all good entrepreneurs need to be able to delegate) and most important of all, keep this book handy, don't let it gather dust on a shelf.

Share your experiences with others

One of the most impressive characteristics I have noticed among exceptionally successful business entrepreneurs is their very honest and genuine desire to share their knowledge and experiences. I think this is something we should all be prepared to do. Most successful people will be the first to tell you they have made every mistake imaginable (and generally they have made them a number of times over). But the fact that they make these mistakes—which are sometimes quite devastating but they manage to pick themselves up, brush the dust off and then give it another go—is an incredible testimony to their fortitude and conviction. There is nothing more inspirational and motivational than hearing how someone overcame adversity and turned it into success; but for the person telling the story, it is often not that remarkable.

From my own experience I am constantly surprised by people who want to know my story and background. I grew up as an orphan, had a very unusual life, did a range of jobs as diverse as commercial diving and selling encyclopaedias door-to-door, owned and operated many businesses, I certainly don't feel my life was extraordinary—but other people do. And even more importantly, they use it to motivate themselves. So I am happy to tell my story and hope that it helps other people to achieve their dreams and aspirations. I feel we all have a very interesting story to get out and inspire others. We have all had a diverse array of experiences that have made us who we are today and these should be exchanged. Pass on your experiences and knowledge of business and life and you will enjoy the satisfaction of helping other people.

Always think big (how big is up to you)

What is the difference between the person who opens and runs a successful pizza restaurant and the person who opens and runs a chain of pizza restaurants around the world? I believe it is all in the thinking process. If you think big you can be big but most of us get too busy doing what we do to let thoughts about where we are going manifest and form. There is nothing wrong with being a small successful business but likewise there is nothing wrong with building that small successful business into a hugely successful big business.

Now I know there will be some people reading this who will feel there are a multitude of limitations that prevent them from world domination (in the nicest possible way) but from my own experiences and observations of entrepreneurs there is little doubt that those who aim high and think big tend to achieve more.

I personally have a series of big plans, which I have broken into timeframes. For example, in the short-term, I would be happy to pay off my credit cards (like most of us); longer term, I want to sell a million books. Both plans are significant to me and I believe I will do them, even if I am not certain which is harder to achieve. I have a list of about ten significant goals and when I read the longer term ones my analytical brain goes into seizures, but I honestly and sincerely believe I will achieve them.

Think big and go for it.

What can you do today?

What are your long-term plans and ambitions for your business? How much money do you want to earn? Make a list of these goals and don't let your mind put limitations on the size of the goal—if you want to earn one million dollars per year, put it on the list. If you want to expand globally, put it on the list. Keep this list handy, perhaps stick it on the mirror in the bathroom or inside your diary or on the cover of your cheque book. Regardless of where you put it, read it regularly and you will start to move in the direction of achieving these goals.

It's not that serious—have some fun

I am a very firm believer that business should be fun. Sure there are plenty of times when this is easier said than done, but some businesses just seem to lack any joy at all. I can't imagine working in an environment like that for hours on end, day after day, month after month. I think some people confuse professionalism with being serious. It is not unprofessional to have a workplace where people like to laugh and enjoy themselves. As a customer it is much more enjoyable to walk into a light, friendly, energetic environment than a serious, gloomy and uncomfortable environment.

Fun takes many different shapes but I believe very strongly that it should be welcomed into all businesses and I do believe it is a key component of many of the leading winning businesses I have observed. For me it is a real joy to see modern entrepreneurs, such as Richard Branson, who are such key advocates of promoting fun for staff and customers. Sure we all have stressful times, we all have to balance money, deal with unhappy customers, manage staff problems and a host of other everyday issues, but it really isn't that serious. Have some fun at work, encourage other people to do likewise and you and your business will enjoy the benefits for many years to come.

What can you do today?

Make up a list of five things you could do to introduce more fun into your workplace. If you struggle to find five things, ask your staff or ask your customers. There is nothing wrong with asking other people for ideas. Once you have your list, turn it into a reality and introduce these new ideas into your business.

'Sooner or later, those who win are those who think they can.'
Richard Bach, author of *Jonathan Livingston Seagull*

1 | Start with an impressive corporate image

What exactly is corporate image? It is a term that is often thrown into marketing spiels and books but what does it mean and why is it so important? Well the best way to describe corporate image is that it is the look and feel of your business to potential customers or how your business appears from the outside looking in. For many business people too much attention is focused looking the other way—from the inside out. But if the customers are not walking in the door, your corporate image could be to blame.

Your corporate image tells the story of your business. It explains what you do and it positions you against your competitors. There is a lot of psychology associated with corporate imaging—certain words evoke emotional responses; some colours reflect pricing, for example black and gold are generally associated with cheaper products or services; and the use of particular fonts or styles of lettering can make a business look old or modern, professional or amateurish. Having a good corporate image starts with the name and should permeate through the entire business. Most winning businesses have very good corporate images, regardless of their size. The issues covered in this section include:

1 Is your business name telling the right story?
2 Do you have a logo and if you do, is it the right one?
3 What is your tag line?

#1 Is your business name telling the right story?

Choosing the right name for your business is a tough decision. For many new businesses this is often a major stumbling block. What name should you use? Before we look at choosing the right name I want to spend a few moments talking about changing your business name.

Over time all businesses evolve. The name you started out with may no longer be applicable to what you do. Many business owners are very hesitant to change their business name if they have had it for a while because they feel they will lose their current customers. I have done a lot of corporate makeovers and have recommended businesses make quite dramatic changes, often including changing the business' name. Not once has this had a negative impact, in fact, quite the opposite: customers like to see a business is changing and evolving, it shows it is progressive and energetic. Large corporations reinvent themselves regularly and their customers almost expect it.

Don't underestimate your customers' ability to cope with change. From my experience they are better at dealing with it than most business owners. From here you need to decide if your business name really does represent what you truly do. If it does, excellent; if it doesn't, it might be time to make a change.

So what name do you change it to? There are lots of options. You can choose a clever name, you can choose a simple descriptive name or you can choose a combination of both. Some people like to invent their own word. All are fine options but, remember, if you choose a clever name or a non-descriptive name, you will need to spend more money promoting and branding the business to let prospective customers know exactly what product or services you are selling.

One example I worked on recently was for a florist. This business was well-known and established but it had a similar name to all the other florists in the same region. They mentioned the word florist, flowers or bridal in their names. Looking through the Yellow Pages made it really difficult to pick any one name out because they were all basically the same. After a creative session we came up with the name 'Buds'. A short, simple, modern name that reflected the owner's style and beliefs perfectly. They now had a name that was easy to remember, distinctive and fresh. Their business never looked back.

The decision you need to make is: do you want to be more interesting or more functional. I am certainly not advocating either, just explaining the choices. Ideally, coming up with something in the middle, a creative but explanatory style of name, is the easiest to build a brand around and to let customers know what you do.

Whatever your business name is or whatever name it is going to become, getting customers to use the business quickly is the difference between losing money over a short time or over a long time.

What can you do today?

Review your business name. Does it truly represent what you do? Is it well known? Is it right for the direction you are planning to take your business? If it is great, this is still a good exercise to do. If it isn't, now is the time to do something about it. Start planning your new business name and how you will go about changing it. Put some thought into it, ask customers, staff, friends and family, but make your own decision. Remember, resistance to change will always be there but this resistance needs to be overcome for the long-term growth and success of your business.

#2 Do you have a logo and if you do, is it the right one?

A logo is simply a graphical image used to promote your business. For some businesses it is a symbol of some sort, for others it is just the name in a stylised font and for some it is a combination of both. Logos are excellent tools for carrying a unique theme through your business and this is the very essence of a good corporate image.

Logos need to be distinctive and unique to your business. In one of my businesses I use a 'splat' in lime green. Ironically getting a good splat, like a paint splotch, is quite difficult, but the end result is very memorable—the message is: if you use my business we will make an impact on your business. A simple message but one that has worked extremely well. All of our promotional material, stationery, signage and websites use the logo to carry through our corporate image.

One of my major gripes with many modern, smaller businesses is the lack of quality logos or, worse, logos designed at home by someone who really has no idea what they are doing. If you are starting a new business, allocate a budget to developing a good logo. If you are in business and you haven't got a logo or you have a pretty ordinary logo, today may be the day to commission a graphic designer to come up with one that is memorable and distinctive.

Winning businesses have good logos and strong corporate images—because they know how important they are. Think about the logos of companies you deal with. Look through newspapers or magazines and check out the logos of the larger organisations. There is nothing stopping any sized business from having a strong, corporate image. Those that do will reap the rewards.

When deciding on which graphic designer to use, contact a few. Most have websites these days where you can check out their past logo designs. Try to find one whose style you like and ideally show them what type of logos you like. Negotiate a price up front so you know how much it will cost. Remember also that you will need to incorporate the new logo on your stationery and promotional material, so you may wish to plan the introduction of a new logo when your current stocks are low.

If you are changing your existing logo, make a big deal of it. Let your customers and suppliers know, take ownership of it and be proud of your new corporate image.

What can you do today?

If you haven't got a logo, get one! If you have one and it is tired, amateurish or no longer current, get cracking on developing a new one.

#3 What is your tag line?

A tag line is basically a few simple words that make a statement about your business. All businesses can use a tag line and the best advice I can give about choosing one is that it should answer the customer's question, 'Why should I use your business?' And keep it short and sharp.

Trends come and go, tag lines go in and out of fashion like colours, but I think they have considerable merit. Tag lines can be altered as your business changes or as the market in which you do business changes. Like choosing a name for your business, trying to define a simple tag line is not an easy task but the two should go hand in hand.

I recommend buying a book called *More words that sell* if you are looking for inspiration to help you with determining a tag line. This excellent publication is used extensively by most advertising agencies, marketing companies and copywriters looking for words on a daily basis.

What can you do today?

If you have a tag line, review and assess whether it still works. If you haven't got one, get one! Go out right now and purchase a copy of *More Words That Sell* and get those creative juices flowing. Run a competition among your staff or customers for ideas or ask your family, friends or business network for advice.

#4 Consistency and the power of branding

Branding is one of those words we hear a lot. 'Developing a brand', 'building a brand', 'brand value' and so on. Most people think branding is applicable only to large corporations but it isn't. It is equally important for small businesses.

Any business can build a brand. Put simply this means when a consumer sees your company name (and logo) they have a positive perception about the business. This is one of the most appealing aspects of buying a franchise—you are purchasing an accepted brand name that consumers will hopefully already know and have a positive opinion about. Clearly it takes time to build a brand and to develop brand awareness but we all need to do it.

The real key to branding is consistency: sending a consistent message through your advertising, corporate image and look of your business. This affects the appearance of your business and all areas where your business interacts with consumers.

Consistency is controlled by systems—having the right mechanisms in place to ensure all aspects of your business are consistent is the starting point. Later in this chapter I discuss how to control your brand and assign an individual to this task, but the term consistency in all aspects of the business needs to be driven from the top.

Now I know I have also discussed that change is a good thing in corporate imaging but I would like to clarify this. Having a current, relevant and impressive corporate image is essential to making a winning business. If yours doesn't achieve these goals then it needs to be changed and your customers will adapt. But when the change is made, you need to build your corporate image and your brand with consistency in all that you do.

What can you do today?

Have a look around your business and all that is involved with it. In what areas could you become more consistent in your branding? Make a list and start working through them one by one.

#5 Have you got a good corporate colour?

A big part of a strong corporate image is having a strong corporate colour. This means there is generally one dominant colour used in all aspects of your corporate image. This dominant colour is used consistently in everything you do and it forms the basis of the business' promotional material. As an example, I recently worked on a corporate image change for a training company specialising in offering human resources advice to remote areas throughout Australia and Asia. The colour we recommended they use was a deep red/brown ochre, which reflects the colour of the desert. This colour is used on their stationery, their sign writing, their promotional material, their website and their staff uniforms, and it has proven very successful. Their clients look at the colour and clearly relate it to remoteness.

Different colours evoke different emotions and it is important to choose an appropriate colour for your business. Darker colours tend to give a stronger, more established feel, hence a lot of law firms and accountants use dark blues, browns and even black as their corporate colour. Lighter colours tend to reflect a more modern look and feel and they are often favoured by businesses in the creative fields. This is an area where you need to take the advice of a good graphic designer. Decide what image you want to portray and then get them to turn it into a colour.

Colours, like most aspects of corporate branding, can go in and out of fashion so your corporate colours will need to be changed periodically. Just like a logo, they have a finite life span. Make sure the colour you choose can be used consistently in all printing and advertising as some colours are harder and more expensive to reproduce. Orange is one prime example of this; you can end up with a lot of variations which may erode the overall strong and consistent image you are trying to portray.

What can you do today?

If you have a corporate colour, evaluate if it is still appropriate and correct for what you do. If you don't have a specific corporate colour, choose one, ideally with the help of a professional such as a graphic designer.

#6 Who controls your corporate image?

Believe it or not there are companies that specialise in controlling corporate image. These are generally used by large organisations, such as hotel chains, and their role is to be a central point of reference to approve promotional material and advertising for the individual operators within the chain, ensuring all material is consistent with the determined corporate image. This creates a very professional and consistent corporate image and makes sure consumers are being sent the right message.

On a smaller scale, keeping control of your corporate image is equally as important. Over time it can easily start to erode as different fonts are introduced, the colours of the logo start to vary and the layout of promotional material differs each time it is produced. Ideally one person should be used to control all aspects of your corporate image. Their job is to:

- make sure the logo appears in the right format every time
- make sure the colours used are correct and consistent
- ensure the same font is used in promotional material
- ensure the format of details, such as telephone numbers and addresses, is consistent
- sign off on all proofs for advertising and promotional material
- control the use of words to make sure of consistency of copy
- keep copies of all promotional material and advertisements to form a historical library
- control the use of images—for example, always send copies to avoid losing originals.

What can you do today?

Decide how you will control your corporate image and, most importantly, who will control your corporate image.

#7 There comes a time when you need to review your corporate image

Corporate images need to change. Over time they become dated, they lose their impact and to be honest they can often start to look amateurish. There is no set period of time between corporate image changes, it is more a matter of realising when the existing image has had its day and no longer truly represents the business. A lot of businesses struggle with making changes to corporate image—I see this in my work every day. There is an underlying concern that if they change their corporate image they may lose customers. I am not sure if this is a general resistance to change or a genuine belief that their customers could go somewhere else simply because the business introduces a new logo or even a new name.

The reality is that customers like to see businesses changing their corporate image—it shows the business is innovative and keeping up with the times. It shows that the business owners are proud of their business and they are prepared to reinvest in it. I have never, ever, instituted a new corporate image that hasn't been a very positive step in the history of a business. A new corporate image reinvigorates everyone—the business owners, the staff and even the customers. It is in its own right a sign of business success.

Another common mistake I see is the business owner who has developed their own logo and corporate image on their home PC—and they think it is sensational. Sure, sometimes people can develop great logos at home, but more often than not the end result is a long way from the desired professional result and the business' corporate image is terrible.

Spend some money and get a professional logo developed, and get the right advice on the use of colours and the design of promotional material. Saving a few dollars on the design of a strong corporate image is not a smart move and in most cases it ends up being a false economy as the business struggles to attract customers from the start.

What can you do today?

Have a good long hard look at your existing corporate image, specifically your logo, your sign writing and your promotional material. Compare it to your competitors'— and be brutally honest. Ask your business associates, staff and customers if they think it needs to be updated and ask them for an honest and candid opinion. It might be fine, but it might be time to set the wheels in motion to start developing your new corporate image. If you do need some changes made, contact your local graphic designer and make an appointment for them to come in and show you what they can do.

#8 Corporate imagery in advertising

Is your corporate image accurately recreated in your advertising? For many businesses, advertising is done on an ad hoc basis, with no real direction. The end result can be that the advertising does not carry the corporate image through. This means it is harder for potential customers to form an association between your advertising and your business.

Just like all aspects of corporate imaging, your advertising should be consistent and carry the 'look and feel' of your business. Over time this helps to build the effectiveness of your advertising—people see your advertisements and recognise straight away that they relate to your business.

Look at the advertising done by large corporations. You will clearly see that their advertising follows a distinct format designed to be easily recognisable as belonging to them. It is important to overcome the urge to change your advertisements a lot simply for the sake of it. Consumers are bombarded with thousands of advertising messages every day and for advertising to really work it needs time to sink in. If you send a constantly changing message or a confusing message, where the consumer has to try and figure out who the advertisement belongs to, they will simply switch off.

Spend a few minutes looking through your local newspaper and see which advertisements you can identify with a specific company within the first second of looking at it. This is the image we all need to portray. Assess what makes the advertisement so easily recognisable. The colours used, the size of the logo, the type of font used, the pictures used or even the location of the advertisement itself?

If you are not sure how to carry your corporate image through your advertising enlist the services of a good graphic designer. Explain to them exactly what it is you are trying to achieve and they will do the rest.

What can you do today?

Look at your advertising and see if it carries your corporate image through in a consistent manner. If it does, great, but could it be improved? If it doesn't, what can you do to make it happen? Should your logo be more prominent? Should the style of font being used be more consistent or unique? There are lots of ways to build a corporate image into your advertising and a good graphic designer is essential to guide you through the process.

#9 Make sure your team understands your corporate philosophy

All too often the head of an organisation knows where it is going but the tail is never told—it just has to follow blindly and hope for the best. What is your corporate philosophy? Some people may call this your mission statement but I personally think it is more. Where do you see your business being in one year, five years, ten years and even fifty years? Write this down. This may be a simple, one-page document which outlines what your business will look like in the future, including what you will sell, where the business will be located, how many staff you will have, what your role in this organisation will be over this timeframe. These are all good questions that are rarely asked.

Once you know what your vision is take the time to explain it to the people you work with. Share the vision so they know where you are going. They may not be as passionate about it as you but that isn't their job. Even if you don't have any staff, it is good for you to know where you are going to be.

I used to work for a company that had a hundred-year vision in place. This was a huge corporation, but they were very clear on where they were going. They had factored in good times, bad times, wars, political changes, world epidemics, the lot. Quite an amazing document to read and it certainly gave me a sense of belonging to an organisation that knew where it was going. Even if the road ahead had no guaranteed direction, their final destination was very clear.

What can you do today?

Write your own corporate vision—where do you want to be in the future?

#10 Size doesn't matter — unless you let it

This is one of those points that I emphasise a lot in all of my books. Don't let the size of your business prevent you from doing it right. You don't need to be a big corporation to have a good corporate image. I have played a significant role in developing strong corporate images for countless small businesses and, yes, they have invested a significant amount in the image but they have all built much stronger businesses as a result of this investment. In fact, I would go one step further and say that it is much easier for a smaller business to develop a good corporate image than it is for a larger organisation.

Imagine the decision-making process: a small business may have only a couple of people to make the final decision so the process is short; a big corporation can have an endless decision-making process that will make the task almost impossible and often it is, hence any change takes a long time to develop. Costs are proportional. Developing a new logo for a large multi-national corporation can cost almost one million dollars for the design alone; for a small business it can be as little as a few hundred dollars.

Good entrepreneurs know the value of looking the part and they realise that investing in a good corporate image is just one of the steps involved in building a successful business.

What can you do today?

Do you find yourself placing limitations on the development of your business because you fall into the small business category? If you do, put a sign on your wall saying, 'Being a small business is my biggest advantage'.

Action pages

Things I need to do to make my business more successful.
1 Is your business name telling the right story?
Action required right now

. . . .

. . . .

. . . .

. . . .

Completed (date, time and by whom)

. . . .

. . . .

2 Do you have a logo and if you do, is it the right one?
Action required right now

. . . .

. . . .

. . . .

. . . .

Completed (date, time and by whom)

. . . .

. . . .

3 What is your tag line?
Action required right now

. . . .

. . . .

. . . .

. . . .

. . . .

Completed (date, time and by whom)

....

....

4 Consistency and the power of branding
Action required right now

....

....

....

....

Completed (date, time and by whom)

....

....

5 Have you got a good corporate colour?
Action required right now

....

....

....

....

Completed (date, time and by whom)

....

....

6 Who controls your corporate image?
Action required right now

....

....

....

....

Completed (date, time and by whom)

....

....

7 There comes a time when you need to review your corporate image
Action required right now

....

....

....

....

Completed (date, time and by whom)

....

....

8 Corporate imagery in advertising
Action required right now

....

....

....

....

Completed (date, time and by whom)

....

....

9 Make sure your team understands your corporate philosophy
Action required right now

....

....

....

....

Completed (date, time and by whom)

. . . .

. . . .

10 Size doesn't matter—unless you let it
Action required right now

. . . .

. . . .

. . . .

. . . .

Completed (date, time and by whom)

. . . .

. . . .

Brainstorming page

Use this page to write notes, comments, ideas or things to do regarding the preceding section. The aim is to improve your business a little every day, to make it more successful and for you to enjoy being an entrepreneur.

....

....

....

....

....

....

....

....

....

....

....

....

....

....

....

....

....

....

....

....

....

....

....

'Any fool can criticize, condemn, and complain—
and most fools do.'
Dale Carnegie

2 | Building strong relationships

To succeed in business you are going to need to build strong relationships with a lot of different people. These relationships will help your business grow, they may help you through difficult times and they will also bring a lot of enjoyment to your business life. Like any relationship, they need to be built over time and with mutual trust. This section deals with building relationships to help you succeed in your entrepreneurial life. The topics covered include:

\# 11   Who do you want to have a strong relationship with?
\# 12   Always check references of potential suppliers
\# 13   Take the time to get to know the people you want to build a relationship with
\# 14   Loose lips sink ships and sometimes businesses
\# 15   Never let a long-term relationship be destroyed over a petty issue

#11 Who do you want to have a strong relationship with?

A very distinct observation I have made of successful businesses is that the owners are generally very good at building relationships with everyone they deal with. This includes their staff, their customers, their suppliers, their landlords, their bank and their professional advisers, such as lawyers and accountants. These people clearly understand that to create a successful business it takes more than one individual—it takes a team or a network with many components, each equally important.

Often entrepreneurs can overlook some relationships or not really give them the attention they need. One example that comes to my mind in this respect is banking. Like most people I assumed that the days of having a relationship with your bank manager were long gone. I had been with one of the big banks for many years and never really considered changing because I thought all banks were the same. This caused me a lot of problems: I struggled to get an overdraft, I didn't have a personal contact who could advise me on various financial matters and I really looked at banking as an irritation rather than a relationship-building opportunity.

That all changed when I was approached by a small boutique bank called The Cairns Penny Savings & Loans. This bank had been operating for over a hundred years but I didn't really know much about it. My firm was commissioned to develop a Strategic Marketing Plan and a new logo and corporate image for the bank, which we did. During this process I got to learn a lot about this impressive business and before long I had moved my accounts to them. All of a sudden I had a bank manager who not only knew my name, he also took an active role in my business and continues to do so. He is one of my unofficial mentors—an honest and open man who has helped my business to grow—and I will be grateful to him forever.

The point I am trying to make here is that we shouldn't necessarily believe everything we read, in this case, about banks. They are certainly not all the same and the opportunity does exist to forge a relationship if you can find the right person. The same applies to virtually everyone you deal with, but you have to be open-minded to let a relationship form—it takes trust and effort. Every time a customer comes into your business they are putting their trust and faith in you; that you will meet their expectations. If you do they will keep coming back. If you work with your suppliers to develop a mutually beneficial relationship, they will reciprocate.

Just as it is important to try and build relationships there are bound to be some people who you just can't deal with or meet their expectations. In this case there will be no relationship and that is okay. Let it go and move on; hopefully these situations will be minimal.

Make the effort and put some energy and thought into the cogs that make your business go around and determine the benefits to you and to them of your relationship being stronger.

What can you do today?

Make a list of the people who form the network that is your business. Beside these people or companies, rate your current relationship. Look at the ones that need improving and make a plan that outlines how you will make these relationships stronger.

#12 Always check references of potential suppliers

Good suppliers are an important part of the overall running of a successful business. Having a strong relationship with them is important and a good start will help the relationship grow in a positive manner.

When setting up accounts with suppliers it is very likely they will want to do a check on your business to make sure you are able to pay their bills. You will probably have to supply a lot of your personal details, trade references verifying your business is good at paying its bills and a personal guarantee from the business owners or directors, which means if the business goes bankrupt they will be personally liable for any outstanding monies owed.

I think it is equally important you know your suppliers are reputable and most importantly that they will deliver what they say they will. Clearly you don't have the same financial risk as the supplier does when dealing with your business but it is important for you to do some homework and establish that this will be a good relationship for your business and ultimately your customers.

Based on this I recommend that when setting up accounts you ask the supplier to give you the names of some of their customers who can verify they will deliver what they promise when they promise it. Many companies will not do this and that often makes me wonder why not? What are they hiding? They want all of your details but they won't give you any of theirs. Not a fair transaction if you ask me.

If your suppliers let you down, you will probably end up letting your customers down. Your customers won't blame the supplier, they will blame you, and this can affect the long-term success of your business.

What can you do today?

Make it a policy in your business that any new suppliers must supply references you can check to make sure they will deliver according to their promises. If they won't do this, find another supplier—there are plenty out there.

#13 Take the time to get to know the people you want to build a relationship with

Building relationships takes time. Once you identify the people or the businesses that you want to build relationships with you also need to allocate time to get to know them. Now I am not suggesting you move in with them, just that in the course of your daily business you find out a little more about them.

People who are good at building relationships are often good at building businesses. They are genuinely interested in the people they deal with. They take the time to get to know them and by showing an interest the relationship grows naturally anyway.

Think about the people who come into your business on a daily basis and perhaps have done so for years. What do you know about them? For example, the courier who has been picking up and dropping off deliveries for the past twelve months, do you even know their name, where they live, what they did before they became a courier, what they like to do on weekends or what their plans are for the future? Today's courier could be tomorrow's customer.

Spend a little time to get to know the people you do business with and do it sincerely. They will respond in a positive manner and your interactions will be more enjoyable for both parties. They are more likely to go the extra mile if you need them to. They are also more likely to tell other people about your business. All of a sudden you will have another free sales rep promoting your business.

What can you do today?

Think about the people you want to build a relationship with. Pick one and get to know them a little better. Do this with one person every week and enjoy how the relationship (and your business) grows.

#14 Loose lips sink ships and sometimes businesses

While I am advocating the importance of building relationships there needs to be very clear boundaries established. In most business relationships there should be limits on what information you pass on or talk about as there is always the possibility the person you are talking to is going to walk out of your business and into your competitors' and tell them everything. I don't want to sound paranoid, but I have personally experienced this.

I once spoke to a supplier about a project I was tendering for. I discussed prices and the outline of my tender only to find out that a last-minute submission by a competitor got the job because they were cheaper. I did a little research and found out that the brother of my supplier worked at the competitors' business. A coincidence? Not likely, even though that can be the nature of doing business. I learned a valuable lesson from this and moved on, but since then I have been much more cautious about what I tell people.

Further to this a lot of people confide in me about their business. What would happen to my reputation if I didn't honour their trust and started giving away their trade secrets? This is a quick way to develop an unethical reputation.

So in short, build relationships but keep your cards a little close to your chest. No matter how close the relationship appears to be, there are some things that should not be shared as your integrity is on the line.

What can you do today?

Think about how much information you or your staff pass on. Is it too much? Do your staff have clearly defined boundaries on what information they can share and what information is considered confidential and not to be given out for any reason? If not, today is the day to clarify this point.

#15 Never let a long-term relationship be destroyed over a petty issue

All too often a very strong relationship can be ruined over a very small issue. Things can go wrong in business, we all know that, but don't let a perfectly good relationship suffer or end because of an issue that in the scheme of things is quite petty.

If you have a great relationship with a supplier and they mess up on one shipment, they deserve another chance. After all, everyone makes mistakes and while they are embarrassing they are generally not the end of the world.

I deal with a lot of printers and this seems to be a trade where things can go wrong. I have been dealing with the same firm for over ten years and nine out of ten jobs run perfectly. Every once in a while I have to sit them down and read them the riot act, but they handle it very well. Any problems that exist are sorted out quickly and efficiently and we get back to business as usual. If the problem is their fault, they will always cover any costs or print extra quantities to give to my clients as a way of apologising for what has gone wrong.

On a similar note I have a long-standing relationship with a stationery company. We buy a lot of stationery and I have been dealing with this same small business for many years. I could probably get my supplies cheaper elsewhere but in this case my relationship is more valuable. They offer exceptional service and I am prepared to pay for that. I have competing stationery suppliers calling my office every other day trying to get my business but it would take a lot more than cheaper prices to move my business away from my existing supplier. I believe this is an important point to pass on to your staff.

Often people get a little crazed when they are promoted or are new to a position. They try to flex their muscles. This can result in good relationships built over many years being destroyed without the business owner even being aware that it is happening. Life is too short to get stressed and bent out of shape every time something goes wrong. Work with the people you have good relationships with and your business will enjoy the benefits.

What can you do today?

Think about the relationships you have in your business. Would they survive a petty dispute? Have you lost a good relationship because of a small issue that got out of hand? Think about how you would handle the same situation in the future and keep this thought in the back of your mind for the next time a petty situation threatens a good relationship.

Action pages

Things I need to do to make my business more successful.
 # 11 Who do you want to have a strong relationship with?
Action required right now

....
....
....
....

Completed (date, time and by whom)

....
....

 # 12 Always check references of potential suppliers
Action required right now

....
....
....
....

Completed (date, time and by whom)

....
....

 # 13 Take the time to get to know the people you want to build a relationship with
Action required right now

....
....
....
....
....

Completed (date, time and by whom)

....

....

14 Loose lips sink ships and sometimes businesses
Action required right now

....

....

....

....

Completed (date, time and by whom)

....

....

15 Never let a long-term relationship be destroyed over a petty issue
Action required right now

....

....

....

....

Completed (date, time and by whom)

....

....

Brainstorming pages

Use these pages to write notes, comments, ideas or things to do regarding the preceding section. The aim is to improve your business a little every day, to make it more successful and for you to enjoy being an entrepreneur.

....

....

....

....

....

....

....

....

....

....

....

....

....

....

....

....

....

....

....

....

....

....

....

....

....
....
....
....
....
....
....
....
....
....
....
....
....
....
....
....
....
....
....
....
....
....
....
....
....
....

'You can't build a reputation on what you're going to do.'
Henry Ford

3| Make sure the foundations of your business are strong

Most businesses evolve over time. There isn't a lot of structure or planning, the needs of the business influence any changes. As it grows the operation is modified and hopefully becomes more successful. But if you can build your business on strong foundations, the future is much more certain and the overall likelihood of the business doing well is greatly increased.

This doesn't mean that if you have been running your business for a while and the foundations are not strong you are doomed — in fact far from it. What it means is that for long-term success and your peace of mind, you have the opportunity to go back and do some work on your business foundations to dramatically strengthen them. From my own experience this means tidying up a lot of issues that have been lingering in the too-hard basket for too long. It is incredibly liberating to actually address the issues that have been nagging away in the back of your mind, but generally there has never been a good time to address them until today.

The topics covered in this section are:

16 Making your business bigger than one person
17 Write a Business Plan—or get someone to write one for you

18   Understanding the importance of systems
19   Understanding finances—taking control of your business
20   Keeping good records always pays off in the long run

#16 Making your business bigger than one person

Most businesses have a product champion, key person, hero or some other similar kind of person. This simply means that one person is driving the machine and it's their passion that propels the business forward. In the early stages of a business this is very normal and a natural starting point. That is why there are so many people running their own small business. But for a business to grow and have longevity it really needs to be bigger than one person.

Now when I say this I don't mean you need to have more than one person involved, I mean the business needs to appear more like a business than an individual. If you don't build your business in this manner the end result can be that the product champion is left a battered and broken wreck by the side of the entrepreneurial highway. Let's use a mechanic as an example.

Bill Smith is an excellent mechanic. He starts his own workshop called 'Bill Smith's Really Excellent Mechanic Shop'. Before long the customers are streaming in, asking for Bill Smith. He does the job and they are very happy. They keep coming back, and they tell all of their friends. Bill Smith gets busier and busier but a strange thing starts to happen. As he employs mechanics to help him out, his customers make it clear they only want him to work on their car because he always does such a good job. No matter how much he protests and sells the skills of his employees his customers are adamant. Bill Smith ends up working more and more hours to meet his customers' expectations. He has no time to focus on the running of his business or his life outside of the business and slowly his world starts to fall apart. Bill Smith ends up burnt out and exhausted. His business is in a mess and his customers leave in droves. Clearly a sad story that started out much nicer than it ended.

Unfortunately it is a common story. Of course the biggest irony is that this generally only happens to people who are very good at what they do. If Bill Smith had set his business up as 'The Really Excellent Mechanic Shop', where Bill was the owner but he had a team of 'really excellent mechanics', his clients would have had a very different perception. They no longer had to deal with the main man, they simply had to deal with one of the 'really excellent mechanics'. This is a shift in perception that enables the business to grow without being so dependent on the one person.

If you are happy to build your business to a size that is manageable by one person and you have the ability to say no to customers, your business doesn't need to be bigger than one person. But if you have aspirations of building and one day selling your business, it is a really good idea to make it bigger than one person as soon as you can.

So how do you make your business bigger than one person? Think about the name of the business. As much as it can be a good idea to use your name to get the business going it can end up being a liability. Let your customers deal with other people in the business, and make sure you talk up the other people. Show your customers that you are a team. Even if it is a small team, it is a team nevertheless and their needs will be met equally by anyone who is a part of that team. Make sure your business has a strong corporate image (see Section 1) so the customer expects there to be other people involved. Most importantly, let go of the reins a little and let the people you work with step up to the plate. You may be surprised at the results.

What can you do today?

Think about what you need to do to make your business bigger than one person. Is it a matter of changing your business name or starting to raise the profile of the other people working with you? If you are not sure, ask your staff, your customers or your business mentors and associates. Letting go is often the hardest part of this process.

#17 Write a Business Plan—or get someone to write one for you

It's easy for a business to blunder along under its own steam and momentum, not really having any significant direction or plan. These kinds of businesses are a worry. The best comparison I have is that it is like driving around without your headlights on at night. You can kind of make out the shapes on the road, and you will probably be able to miss most of the hazards, but eventually you're going to hit something—odds on, it will hurt, a lot. A Business Plan is the headlights of the business. It gives you direction and focus and in many ways it is a map to guide you forward.

In very simple terms a Business Plan looks at the following:

- where the business has come from
- where the business is heading
- what the business needs to avoid
- how the business will get to where it is going
- how to know when the business has arrived.

Getting a Business Plan done is not a cheap exercise, nor should it be. It is a significant document for any business and you tend to get what you pay for. You can buy a host of books that will tell you how to write your own Business Plan but personally I am an advocate of getting someone else to write it for you. Get a professional to evaluate your business. A fresh pair of eyes really does make a huge difference. I sat down a hundred times to write my own Business Plan and I never got past the title page. I am too close. I then paid a reputable company to write one for me and it is excellent. They identified issues and made recommendations that I would never have even thought of, let alone realised, as potential hazards or opportunities.

My business has clear direction and focus and every week I sit down and review my Business Plan to make sure I am on track to achieve what I want to. It is a very valuable document and I have no doubt it was worth every cent.

What can you do today?

If you haven't got a Business Plan, maybe today is the day to get one organised. Talk to your local government-run business development agency. Often there are excellent grants available to help businesses fund a professionally produced Business Plan.

#18 Understanding the importance of systems

Systems are all the talk of the business world these days and have been ever since a very smart man called Michael Gerber wrote the very famous book *The E myth*. He wasn't the first person to come up with the idea of systems, they have been around for thousands of years, but he was one of the first people to be able to describe how important they are for the long-term success and sustainability of a business.

The concept of systems is simply to add structure to the day-to-day processes that happen within a business. McDonald's is the easiest business to use as an example here. The entire organisation is built on systems from the bottom up to the very top. Systems mean there is a very clear procedure to follow to do anything within a business. At McDonald's there is a system or a checklist for pre-opening in the morning, for getting the kitchen started, for greeting the customers, for making the burgers, for putting the food on the tray, for thanking the customer and for cleaning up after the customer. Anyone can learn a specific system within a matter of minutes. This makes training easy and it means a very high level of consistency in the business—and customers love consistency.

Systems can be applied to virtually every business at some level. The biggest problem is that most entrepreneurs are too busy running their business to document the systems they use and they tend to be kept in their heads. The hard part is to get the information out of their head and into the heads of their staff. The end result is generally barely controlled chaos and inconsistent service—which customers hate.

Systemised businesses are very popular. They are appealing to people buying businesses because they can be managed much more easily than non-systemised businesses. That is why franchises are so popular. You get a manual that tells you exactly what to do and when to do it.

Systems are gold. They let you get on with running the business. They are cost conscious because staff can learn their jobs quickly. They provide a mechanism for giving your customers consistent service. They make your business more appealing to buy. There really are no downsides to putting systems in place.

What can you do today?

If you haven't read *The E Myth* by Michael Gerber, go out and grab a copy today. If you read it a while ago, pull it off the shelf, dust it down and read it again. If it is already by your bed and you have read it recently, compile a list of the processes that happen within your business that could be systemised and start doing it. Get your staff involved — often they have a much better idea about how to systemise a business process because they do it all day every day.

#19 Understanding finances—taking control of your business

If you are like me the financial aspect of running the business is a chore. It is much more interesting and enjoyable to be at the business end—doing what you do. I would much rather be developing a marketing campaign for a client than talking margins and profit and loss or cash flow with my accountant. But this can be a little dangerous. If you don't pay enough attention to your business' finances it is very easy to get into a lot of trouble, often before you even realise you are in trouble.

As a business owner and as an entrepreneur the buck stops with you. Not knowing or not understanding your financial position is not a good argument during a tax audit (and if you haven't experienced one of them, boy are you in for a treat).

I strongly recommend two things. Firstly, from now on question your accountant or bookkeeper about what everything in your business' financial statements means no matter how silly you may feel. Get to know the terminology and decide whether you agree your books accurately reflect your business. It really isn't that complicated.

From my experience many accountants aren't that good at communicating so they don't tend to give you good descriptions. In all fairness, they deal with the terms day in day out, so most are second nature to them and perhaps they forget they aren't second nature to us. Make it your business to understand your accounts.

The second recommendation I would make is to enrol in a simple business bookkeeping course so you get to know more about the processes being used in your own business. I am not saying you should do your own bookwork if you don't want to, but at least understand it better. It is very liberating to be able to look at a profit and loss statement and understand what it means. Most people have no idea.

What can you do today?

If you don't understand what your business's financial statements actually mean, make an appointment to get your accountant to explain them to you—it is well worth the expense. Then book yourself in to do a basic bookkeeping course.

#20 Keeping good records always pays off in the long run

I remember my first visit to an accountant. I had three years' worth of business records crammed into three shoe boxes. My poor accountant. Since then I have well and truly learned the lesson of keeping good records.

Quite simply not keeping good records will cost you money, often a lot of money. Basically there are two lots of records that need to be kept in business—money in and money out. Poor records regarding money coming into the business tends to border on tax evasion, or at least avoidance, and taxation departments in all countries tend to be rather down on this subject. Poor record keeping of money going out of the business often means you can't claim justified expenses because you don't have the appropriate receipts or records. So not only do you not get the deduction, the expense is classed as a personal expense and you have to pay tax on it. Whichever way you look at it, poor record keeping does not do a lot towards building a successful business.

Often records can be in such a mess it is hard to know where to start and that itself prevents the entrepreneur from getting their act together. The best thing to do is to bite the bullet and get someone in to help you. Get a professional; odds on they have been through this situation before (and you should check to make sure they have). Generally you will find they can rattle off half a dozen stories of businesses that have been in far worse condition than yours, which really does make you feel a lot better.

Even if you think your records are pretty good, maybe today is a good day to review your systems and record keeping to look for ways to make it even better.

What can you do today?

If you think it is time to dig out the shoe boxes and call an accountant, do it. Get the phone book out or ask your business associates and mentors for a recommendation. Take control of your record keeping today. If you think your records are pretty smart, try to find at least one thing you could be doing better.

Action pages

Things I need to do to make my business more successful.
16 Making your business bigger than one person
Action required right now

. . . .

. . . .

. . . .

. . . .

Completed (date, time and by whom)

. . . .

. . . .

17 Write a Business Plan—or get someone to write one for you
Action required right now

. . . .

. . . .

. . . .

. . . .

Completed (date, time and by whom)

. . . .

. . . .

18 Understanding the importance of systems
Action required right now

. . . .

. . . .

. . . .

. . . .

. . . .

Completed (date, time and by whom)

. . . .

. . . .

19 Understanding finances—taking control of your business
Action required right now

. . . .

. . . .

. . . .

. . . .

Completed (date, time and by whom)

. . . .

. . . .

20 Keeping good records always pays off in the long run
Action required right now

. . . .

. . . .

. . . .

. . . .

Completed (date, time and by whom)

. . . .

. . . .

Brainstorming page

Use this page to write notes, comments, ideas or things to do regarding the preceding section. The aim is to improve your business a little every day, to make it more successful and for you to enjoy being an entrepreneur.

'A banker is a fellow who lends you his umbrella when the sun is shining, but wants it back the minute it begins to rain.'

Mark Twain

4 | Have absolute commitment to your customers

Winning businesses understand the importance of keeping their customers happy. They know they have to exceed their expectations whenever they can. They have to respect their customers and they have to be better than their competitors at delivering high levels of customer service.

Customer service is a big issue and one that is not easy to cover in one section of a book like this, which is aiming to deliver a well-rounded overview of building a successful business. But the topics covered in this section are the most important issues to consider.

21 It's all about respect—if you don't respect your customers don't expect them to come back

22 Never lose touch with your customers

23 Do you over promise and under deliver?

24 The first 30 seconds

25 Talk about customer service to your staff—a lot

26 Reward good customers

27 Keep a notepad in your pocket

28 Time—the one commodity that causes the most grief

29 Customer expectations are changing—we all need to change with them

30 Look at the entire customer service picture—not just little pieces

#21 It's all about respect—if you don't respect your customers don't expect them to come back

It is hard to build a winning business if you don't respect your customers (mind you, plenty of businesses seem to have a good go at it). Respect is a very powerful word when it comes to customers and there are a lot of ways to show respect for your customers. Often though, it is easier to come up with examples of how customers are treated with little or no respect.

What do I mean by respecting your customers? I think there are a number of areas where you can show respect for your customers including:

- respect their time—they shouldn't have to wait for you. Making someone wait in a queue for half an hour is not a sign of respect
- respect the fact that they made a conscious decision to use your business
- respect the fact that their opinions regarding your business are important and appreciated
- respect the fact that if they refer someone else to your business they are showing a significant sign of commitment to your business
- respect the fact that if you fail to meet their expectations they will take their business elsewhere.

Respect for customers has to start at the top. If the people that own the business don't respect their customers it is impossible to expect the staff down the line to show any respect for customers. We all need to have a very clear 'customer commitment statement'. This is very simply a one or two sentence description that captures the essence of your philosophy towards your customers. Anyone involved in your business should be made aware of your customer commitment statement, including your customers.

What can you do today?

Make up your own customer commitment statement and make certain everyone involved in your business and your customers know what it is.

#22 Never lose touch with your customers

I recently attended a presentation by Tom Potter, one of Australia's leading entrepreneurs and the founder of Eagle Boys Pizza, a business with 150 franchises across Australia. It was interesting to note that Mr Potter still takes the time to physically work behind the counter in many of the Eagle Boys Pizza franchises he visits. His reasoning: 'To make certain I never lose touch with our customers.' A lot of business people could learn a valuable lesson from his example.

Personally I believe that anyone who sits on the board of a large company should spend a prerequisite amount of time dealing with customers at the coal face of the business. Too often large companies lose touch with their customers simply because the people making the decisions are too sheltered from the frontline.

In small business we often spend a lot of our time trying to get away from directly dealing with customers because it can be tough, demanding, frustrating and time consuming. I am certainly not saying that every business owner should spend forty hours a week behind the cash register but I do believe every one of them should be communicating with the customers on a regular basis. Depending on the type of business this may mean making a few phone calls each week, or it may mean physically standing on the floor.

From my experience, those businesses where the final decision maker interacts directly with customers on a regular basis tend to offer far greater levels of customer service than those that do not. Don't be afraid to talk to your customers and to ask for their opinions—remember without customers your business would be a very lonely place.

What can you do today?

Consider how you can spend more time with customers to get their feedback and opinions on what your business is doing well and what it could do better.

#23 Do you over promise and under deliver?

In businesses that are overly busy this point poses a challenge. In businesses not so busy, it is unforgivable. Over promising and under delivering is the best way to lose customers as it breaks every customer service rule. Firstly you are building up the customer's expectations, probably higher than they were initially, then you not only fail to meet their expectations, you fail miserably.

It is easy to get pressured into over promising and under delivering. In my industry, everyone wants marketing advice and strategies quickly, but the reality is they take time to prepare. A rushed strategy can be flawed and the end result disastrous for the business concerned. I specifically explain this to my clients at length and I have to be careful to make sure the timeframe I quote to deliver their strategy is realistic and achievable. Once committed, I will move heaven and earth to make sure the very best quality product is delivered on time.

It is better to set a realistic timeframe, one you can achieve, than one you can't possibly achieve, which is guaranteed to end in tears for all the parties concerned.

There are of course many other forms of over promising and under delivering. One of the most obvious is food. We have all seen sensational television advertisements promoting mouth-watering meals, filling us with expectation, only to find the end product is a shrivelled, poor impersonation of what was on the commercial. Likewise, the advertisement may spout on about how your business is valued and how staff will treat you like celebrities, but when you pick up the phone the person on the other end treats you like anything but royalty. Some of this problem is due to the distance between the marketing people and the end product. But as a marketing person I have never had a brief that said to make sure you show our burgers looking soggy and unappetising. The key here is to be honest in your representation of your product or service.

Don't underestimate your customers' intelligence. They know when they are being treated with contempt and they will soon let you know.

What can you do today?

Evaluate your business—are there areas where you over promise and under deliver? Why not make a commitment to end this cycle today.

#24 The first 30 seconds

The first 30 seconds of any business interaction are best considered an interview. A customer forms a lot of opinions in this initial window of opportunity for you. Generally most impressions are done subconsciously with a simple end result being a message from the brain of the customer saying, 'I will come back here again' or, 'I will not come back here again'. Sure this process may take longer in some businesses, but you get the point.

I do a lot of mystery shopper evaluations for various companies. This is where I visit the business as a customer but my job is to evaluate how they could do things better, generally from a customer service perspective. My most common negative comment is that the business fails to impress from the start and that sets the mood for the rest of the interaction.

Make your first business impressions count. If you have a business where people come in off the street, you always need to look impressive, neat, tidy and clean. Your staff need to be well presented and the 'welcome' needs to be honest and sincere. If your business is one where people phone in, the call needs to be answered promptly, and the person answering the call needs to speak clearly and listen to what the caller is saying. They need to be able to answer the queries or direct the caller to someone who can help them (not just put them in a never ending cycle of 'someone else's problem'). If your business' first point of contact is through a brochure in the mail it needs to get the reader's attention quickly and answer the right questions. If the reader has to try and figure out what it is all about, it will end up in the too-hard basket or the bin.

Remember first impressions set the mood for all future interactions and dealings. Make your first 30 seconds as good as they can be and your business will be well and truly on the way to achieving winning status.

What can you do today?

Review your own first 30 seconds. Make a list of five things you could do right now to change your initial contact with a customer from mediocre to magnificent and implement them today. Attention to detail is important here.

#25 Talk about customer service to your staff—a lot

Customer service is an issue that many businesses really struggle to get a handle on. For some people it is simply serving customers quickly and politely, but in reality it goes much deeper.

Earlier in this chapter I talked about the importance of respecting your customers, which I believe is the starting point when it comes to delivering high levels of customer service. While you may respect your customers, the relevance of this is often hard to pass on to your staff.

Most businesses will talk endlessly about sales to staff: is the business reaching its targets, how can sales be improved, how can more customers be attracted and how can they be encouraged to spend more with the business? The topic of customer service is often overlooked, generally because I feel that business owners aren't really sure how to address more than a few very obvious customer service issues.

Customer service should be talked about a lot. It should be debated, it should be reviewed and it should be discussed at every opportunity. This can get a little boring and start to sound like a broken record so it is up to the person doing the talking to be a little innovative.

Buy a book on customer service with lots of great ideas on how to stand out from the crowd by offering exceptional customer service. Without meaning to turn this into a sales pitch, my third book, called *101 Ways to Really Satisfy Your Customers*, is a pretty good starting point. It actually contains 121 very simple and practical ways to improve any business' level of customer service. There are many other books available and most contain excellent tips.

Encourage your staff to make suggestions on how they feel your business' customer service could be improved. Ask your customers for their feedback and recommendations. Talk about these recommendations with your staff and see if they can be implemented. By getting your staff and customers involved the concept of customer service becomes much more tangible.

In short, devote as much time to improving customer service as you do to improving sales and your business will grow naturally as it gains a reputation for offering excellent service.

What can you do today?

Go out today and buy a book on customer service and start to introduce the recommendations to your staff. Don't bombard them with 100 ideas in one hit—introduce one or two at a time and then action them properly.

#26 Reward good customers

Good customers are hard to find and there are plenty of other businesses fighting for them. For this reason it is essential you reward good customers for coming back to your business. There are many ways to show you appreciate your regular customers and most businesses can easily implement either a formal or informal system that will do exactly that.

A formal reward system may be a loyalty card style of programme, where repeat customers receive discounts or special offers whenever they use the business. It may include invitations to special events, access to special products or services or a special incentive after making a certain number of purchases.

An informal system could be something more spur of the moment, where you offer a 'reward' on the spot to a regular customer as your way of saying thank you for their business. My local coffee shop does this very well. Every once in a while the owner will refuse to take my money, saying, 'This one is on the house'. A very nice touch that is most appreciated and, of course, I keep going back for more. I don't expect the freebie but I certainly appreciate it.

What can you do today?

Are you rewarding your regular customers or are you taking them for granted and simply assuming that they will keep coming back? Why not implement either a formal or an informal rewards system for your good customers today?

#27 Keep a notepad in your pocket

Successful business entrepreneurs tend to be very good observers. They have a thirst for knowledge and they are always looking for ways to make their business run better. Whenever they deal with another business they are often evaluating the service they are getting and looking for ideas they can use. The hard part can be remembering all of the good things observed.

As a budding entrepreneur you need to become an observer. Every interaction could possibly contain some valuable idea that you could use to make your business more profitable. However, it is easy to forget your observations in the course of a busy day. If you keep a notepad handy you'll find it takes only a second to jot down a couple of notes for later reference. I do this a lot and subsequently I have notepads all over the place—in my car, on my bedside table, around the house, in my gym bag—I always carry one with me. This may be a bit of an overkill for some, but I have so many things going around in my mind that if I don't write things down it is easy for me to forget them.

I find that when I'm driving, especially long distances, I have this amazing influx of good ideas and I need to write them down then and there. Of course, this means I am forever pulling over to write notes, but it doesn't bother me for a second because by the time I arrive at my destination, I have a pile of new inspirational ideas that can be used in my business or by my clients to make their businesses more profitable.

I have friends who keep small tape recorders in their pockets for the same reason (at least that's what they tell me). Whenever they have a thought they simply pull out the recorder and tape a message to themselves. Many mobile phones have this capacity as well.

To make your business as successful as it can be, be prepared to become an observer of every other business you deal with, from the local newsagency to your bank. Look out for good ideas that you can use in your business.

What can you do today?

Buy yourself some notepads and leave them in readily accessible spots. Alternatively, buy yourself a mini tape recorder or upgrade your mobile. Start to become an observer.

#28 Time—the one commodity that causes the most grief

The one topic sure to spark unanimous agreement in the modern business world is that we are all struggling to find enough time to get everything we need to do done. There are so many different aspects to our lives that demand our time and attention. Often it can all be a little overwhelming. Time, time, time—the greatest commodity which, ironically, we all have the same amount of.

When you look at time from a customer service perspective it is the one area where consumers are unforgiving. If a business wastes their time—look out. Winning businesses realise this and they will do their utmost to make sure their customers' time is treated as the precious commodity it is.

Think about your own frustrations when it comes to time-related customer service issues. Waiting for too long in a restaurant, standing in queues anywhere, waiting around at home for a tradesperson to turn up and make a repair, waiting for someone to call you back and a myriad of other typically time frustrating scenarios. Think of how your mind processes thoughts regarding certain businesses. For example, you might have a favourite coffee shop but you know you have to wait quite a long time for a coffee. Often this will stop you from going there simply because you haven't got the time to stand around waiting for a coffee. After a while you stop going there and so do lots of other people. Sure the business may do well initially, but eventually the owners will wonder where all of the customers have gone.

If you can show your customers that you respect their time they will appreciate it, even if you don't always get it right.

Most businesses have peaks and troughs, when they are busier than usual or quieter than usual, and customers understand this. Most of us eat at restaurants for either lunch or dinner, along with everyone else. So these are the times when you expect to wait a little longer. But when the restaurant is quiet, we expect to be served fast and efficiently.

One of the biggest mistakes I observe with businesses that fail to respect time is that they don't acknowledge the customers who are waiting. No eye contact or recognition is made until the customer is the next one at the counter. So much grief can be overcome by simply smiling at the people waiting and letting them know the wait won't be long. Acknowledge the customer and show them you understand their time is valuable and you are doing your best to serve them quickly.

It all comes back to communication. If you are going to be late, call the customer. If you can't deliver a product on time, let them know.

Look for ways to streamline what you do to speed up the customer service. Often it is the little things that can make businesses serve their customers faster. It might be the layout of the business, if it is a retail style of operation. It might be staffing levels at critical times or it might be the actual sales process itself—maybe it is overly complicated and has too much paperwork. Maybe your staff need to be better trained.

Regardless of the business, find ways to serve your customers as fast as possible and your business will develop a reputation for providing excellent service and more customers will use it.

What can you do today?

Look at the way you serve your customers. Is there any part of the sales process where you could show a greater level of respect for your customers' time by speeding up the system? Look at how other businesses serve their customers and see if you can adopt any of their procedures in your business to speed up your customer service. Today, implement one action that will make a difference and enjoy the difference it makes.

#29 Customer expectations are changing—we all need to change with them

I am an advocate of the importance of improving customer service and the easiest way to do this is to exceed your customers' expectations. The difficult part is that customer expectations are constantly changing and that can make it hard to know where you stand.

There was a time when customer expectations didn't really matter because there were not a lot of options for them to choose from. Cars came in one or two colours, so did suits. Restaurant menus had a handful of choices. When you went to the cinema there was only one movie playing or there was only one channel to watch on the television or listen to on the radio. Those times have well and truly passed.

Choice is one commodity that is certainly not in short demand and everyone wants to succeed by attracting more customers than their opposition. Added to this is the fact that we all have access to far more media than ever before—magazines, newspapers, the Internet, television, radio and a host of other forms of communications—all of them bombarding consumers with marketing and advertising messages. It is well documented that this is the driving force in consumer trends and every advertising agency and marketing professional is trying to find a way to get their product in front of more potential customers. So we, the consumer, are well informed, aware and intelligent, and we have high expectations that are changing constantly.

What does this mean to the average business owner and entrepreneur? It means we can never sit back and be complacent when it comes to meeting our customers' expectations. What works today may not work tomorrow, we need to always be one step ahead of the pack and we need to become better at communicating with our customers. But most importantly, we need to be able to adapt the way we do business to meet these changing expectations.

The age of 'that is the way we always did it' is long gone and the dinosaurs still living in that Jurassic mindset are finding out fast that it is not a sustainable business model. I see a lot more companies failing today after decades of being successful, mostly because they can't change with the times and their customers outgrow them.

What can you do today?

Look at your own business and consider what steps you are taking to ensure you stay at the front of the pack. Make a list of any things you do, 'because that's the way we always do it'. Ask yourself, honestly, whether there is a better way to do it. Let go of the old and welcome in the new and your business will appreciate it.

#30 Look at the entire customer service picture—not just little pieces

Many businesses consider customer service as just the time they are dealing face-to-face with their customers. In reality the entire customer service picture is much bigger. It is often easy to go into a business where the initial greeting from someone behind the counter is excellent, and then everything else that follows falls apart.

I noticed this recently at a huge hardware store that I visited. I was met at the front door by a delightful young lady who sincerely welcomed me to the business and advised me where to go to find what I needed. What a great start. So I trundled off to find the various bits of hardware, which meant nothing to me but they were on my list. From there, the system fell apart: I couldn't find anyone to help me; the staff were clustered in small groups talking to each other and they treated me like an idiot when I asked questions; they then gave me the wrong items and kept me waiting for over an hour before my problems were solved; they got the bill wrong; and they threw my items into the back of my car. Basically, they took my money and kicked me out. Typically this business was being directed by a very old adage, one I have covered in this section: the first 30 seconds are vitally important for the customer to form positive opinions about the business. But this is a waste of time if the entire system falls apart after the first 30 seconds.

Every single business is set up to sell something to someone. If your customer service can be its very best at every level of the business, you will have to fight customers off with a stick (not a good customer service technique I might add). Think much bigger than just the front counter.

For a lot of business owners and managers this is a daunting task. My advice here is to break your business into components and address each one from a customer service perspective. Over time each component will be dealt with and each improvement will lift your overall level of customer service.

What can you do today?

Break your business into components or modules so you can assess and review your level of customer service for each individual part. Then start working your way through the list, coming up with ways to improve the customer service offered in each component. If you are stuck for ideas, get your staff involved (a good idea anyway) and get your customers involved (an even better idea).

Action pages

Things I need to do to make my business more successful.
21 It's all about respect—if you don't respect your customers don't expect them to come back
Action required right now

....

....

....

....

Completed (date, time and by whom)

....

....

22 Never lose touch with your customers
Action required right now

....

....

....

....

Completed (date, time and by whom)

....

....

23 Do you over promise and under deliver?
Action required right now

....

....

....

....

....

Completed (date, time and by whom)

. . . .

. . . .

 # 24 The first 30 seconds
Action required right now

. . . .

. . . .

. . . .

. . . .

Completed (date, time and by whom)

. . . .

. . . .

 # 25 Talk about customer service to your staff—a lot
Action required right now

. . . .

. . . .

. . . .

. . . .

Completed (date, time and by whom)

. . . .

. . . .

 # 26 Reward good customers
Action required right now

. . . .

. . . .

. . . .

. . . .

. . . .

Completed (date, time and by whom)

. . . .

. . . .

27 Keep a notepad in your pocket
Action required right now

. . . .

. . . .

. . . .

. . . .

Completed (date, time and by whom)

. . . .

. . . .

28 Time—the one commodity that causes the most grief
Action required right now

. . . .

. . . .

. . . .

. . . .

Completed (date, time and by whom)

. . . .

. . . .

29 Customer expectations are changing—we all need to change with them
Action required right now

. . . .

. . . .

. . . .

. . . .

Completed (date, time and by whom)

....

....

30 Look at the entire customer service picture—not just little pieces
Action required right now

....

....

....

....

Completed (date, time and by whom)

....

....

Brainstorming pages

Use these pages to write notes, comments, ideas or things to do regarding the preceding section. The aim is to improve your business a little every day, to make it more successful and for you to enjoy being an entrepreneur.

....

....

....

....

....

....

....

....

....

....

....

....

....

....

....

....

....

....

....

....

....

....

....

'People call me a perfectionist, but I'm not. I'm a rightist. I do something until it's right and then I move on to the next thing.'
James Cameron, Academy Award-winning director

5 | Making your workplace unbelievable

This is an interesting section, one that really addresses the differences between mediocre and winning businesses. The place where you conduct your business should be impressive in a lot of different ways. Even if you don't have customers visiting your business, surely it is important for your staff to enjoy coming to work and, hopefully, even love coming to work. The real aim of this section is to identify ways to make your business more appealing to your customers. It covers a range of key issues to achieve this goal and, as a result, your business will stand out as a winning business.

31   Have pride in your workplace (even if you are the only one there)

32   Make your workplace inviting and easy for your customers to visit

33   Don't scrimp on the little things (out with *Women's Weekly* 1972)

34   Offer really good coffee and tea (and nice cups)

35   Just add laughter (in vast amounts and often)

36   Encourage people to bring their personality to work

37   Beware of bad smells

38   Who is in control of the music?

39   Cleanliness is a key component to profitability

40   Make one person the keeper of the workplace

#31 Have pride in your workplace (even if you are the only one there)

When was the last time you walked into a business and went, 'Wow'? My guess would be not recently, but I hope I am wrong. Your workplace should be impressive, even if you are the only person working there.

Having pride in your workplace means it looks clean and tidy, it is organised and it is ready for business. Too many businesses look run down and worn out—often reflecting the feelings of the business owners. The place might look dirty and grubby, the pictures are crooked, the brochures are in messy piles, none of the furniture matches, there is a very strange smell, the carpet is faded, AC/DC is blaring on a cheap stereo and there is no real sign of life—certainly no feeling of energy or enthusiasm from the staff.

Compare this to the concept of walking into a well-lit, freshly painted business, where all the displays are neat and tidy, the staff are wearing clean, ironed uniforms, there are fresh flowers on the counter and a clean smell throughout, everything looks in place and there is gentle background music playing. Much more inviting and memorable.

An excellent idea I promote throughout this book is the concept of becoming a better observer of other businesses. This is a characteristic that I have seen as a common thread in many very successful entrepreneurs—they look at everything. Whenever you go into a business take a moment to look around—what do they do right and what do they do wrong? From here, what could you do better?

I think too many workplaces look shocking, specifically in some industries. They look functional, definitely uninspired and, generally, no one wants to stay there too long. Personally I couldn't imagine working in a place like that. To me, we all spend more time at work than just about anywhere else. I think it is essential my office looks clean, inviting, motivational and welcoming for my customers, my suppliers and my staff—and for me!

It is like the business where the front reception is very impressive but as soon as you walk out back it looks like a bomb has gone off. Have pride in your workplace and it will be reflected in everyone who deals with you. Just getting the compliments from your customers is very rewarding, but the overall financial benefits of having a business that looks like you care about it will be even more rewarding because the customers will want to keep coming back.

What can you do today?

Do you really have pride in your workplace? If you do, congratulations, but now focus on becoming an observer of other businesses to look for ways to make it even better. If your workplace needs an extreme makeover, today is the day to start planning it. Someone needs to take control of the makeover and if you can't do it, find someone who can.

#32 Make your workplace inviting and easy for your customers to visit

If you run a business where the customers come to you, make it inviting and easy for them to not only find the business but also to actually get into the business. While it is important to make the business inviting once the customers are inside, if they can't find it or if it doesn't look appealing enough on the outside to go in, the rest can be a waste of time. To make your business easy for your customers to visit there are a number of issues to consider.

Some businesses are so hard to find that for many time-deprived customers they will simply give up and go elsewhere. Good signage to direct people is certainly essential, and if you tend to use directions quoting a street number it is a wise idea to have that number well signed (in big print, preferably) in a very visible place.

Making it easy for your customer to park is another good tip. I recently visited a large shopping centre that had reconfigured its car park to try and fit more cars in. Unfortunately they had made all of the parking bays much smaller so it was now a tight squeeze to park and it was also very likely your car would get damaged by people opening doors or moving trolleys around the parked cars. Not a good move.

The entrance to your business should also be very clearly marked. It can be frustrating to have to wander around the outside of a business trying to figure out how to get inside. Having a sign of your trading hours in a clearly visible spot also makes it easy for customers to know when the business is open.

To make the entrance inviting it should not be overly cluttered. Creating barriers for people to negotiate can make the business less appealing. This doesn't mean you can't have some products on display outside the business but make sure the access is not blocked.

The front of the business should always be clean and tidy. This should be one of the first jobs done when preparing the business to open up for the day and it should be repeated during the day on a regular basis. I am often surprised at how dirty the front of many businesses are. It doesn't make a good impression and, as discussed elsewhere in this book, first impressions are very important.

Having good lighting is another important issue, especially if your customers visit your business at night. We are all a little more aware and concerned about our personal safety these days and a well-lit premises is far more appealing than one that isn't.

Every business is different, but the principles are the same. Make your business inviting and appealing and your customers will be more likely to come back. It isn't difficult, but like most of the recommendations in this book it needs someone to put a system in place to make sure it is done.

What can you do today?

How easy is it to find your business? How appealing is the entrance? Take a few minutes to walk around it and make a list of things that could be done right now to make it more approachable. Either do those things yourself or put a system in place to make sure they are done on a regular basis throughout the day. If your customers are telling you your business is hard to find, figure out where you can place directional signage and get it happening today.

#33 Don't scrimp on the little things (out with *Women's Weekly* 1972)

Every week I spend $50 on flowers for my reception. We purchase these from the local markets and they always look sensational. I get more comments and compliments regarding these flowers than any other part of the business (I should have opened a florist, not a marketing company). People walking by stick their heads in just to tell us how much they like the flowers. I believe this is a very good investment in my business and I would never even think about not doing it.

We have all experienced a visit to a business where the waiting room is filled with ten-year-old magazines that are tattered and torn, or blank walls, or a tired and dusty plastic plant on the counter. These may seem like little things in the scheme of a business but the little things can make all the difference. You really notice this when you visit a business that pays good attention to detail. It is far more inviting and enjoyable to visit. We tend to expect a business to have old magazines but when they are the latest edition we are pleasantly surprised and it makes an impression.

Whatever your business, if people come to you, paying attention to the details that make it more enjoyable for your customers to visit will impress them. They will tell their friends, even if they are not sure why they like the business. Of course, you need to be able to back up the attention to detail with good products and services, but at least your customers are in the right frame of mind when they visit.

What can you do today?

Make a list of five things that you could do better to make your business more appealing to your customers. This needs to be repeated on a regular basis, and, most importantly, the list is only the start. Actioning the list is the difference between a winning business and a mediocre one.

#34 Offer really good coffee and tea (and nice cups)

If you run a business where your customers tend to spend a little time, you naturally offer them tea and coffee. It really makes a difference if you offer them good coffee and tea and you serve them in nice, clean cups. It reinforces your attention to detail and the value you place on their custom.

Some businesses just fall apart when it comes to this area of service. There isn't any milk, they are out of coffee or, even worse, it is the cheapest coffee available, purchased in giant tins that have been around for ten years, or the cups are dirty and lipstick stained. If you are going to make the offer, be prepared for your customers to say yes. Have good quality coffee, fresh milk, a range of teas—remembering that a lot of people drink herbal teas these days—sugar and sugar substitutes, clean quality cups and a presentable tray to carry it all on.

I am sure that some readers may be thinking, 'Is this really that big a deal?' and my answer is, 'Yes'. Successful businesses are different from their competitors—and the differences are normally the little things. Being committed to making your business better than your competitors' means putting that extra effort and energy into looking after your customers. For those businesses that already do this they know that it works. For those who are unsure, try it and see the response from your customers.

Another good idea includes having good drinking water and clean glasses, or a ready supply of plastic cups. I have several water coolers throughout my office, with one in my boardroom, to make sure any visitor to my office has easy access to quality filtered water. Having a box of tissues in the boardroom and at reception is another simple point that doesn't appear to be a big deal but is another reinforcement of the fact that you care about your customers.

Magnificent businesses care for their customers and they are prepared to show it.

What can you do today?

How can you show your customers that you care? You might already serve really good tea and coffee, but there is bound to be another aspect missing that will in some way show you care. Work out what that one thing is and implement it today.

#35 Just add laughter (in vast amounts and often)

I am a very big advocate of having a lot of fun in your workplace. This is a point which I discussed in the introduction to this book. Having fun is not unprofessional—everyone benefits and people like to be involved.

The most noticeable example I have seen of this in recent times was by a national fresh juice business that has grown to have hundreds of outlets in a very short time—Boost Juice. A visit to one of these stores is like visiting the theatre. The staff have a lot of interaction with each other and they laugh, they have fun, they clown around and they generally seem to be having a pretty good time. As a customer it is very refreshing to watch a group of young, energetic people having fun doing what they are doing. It makes the whole experience far more enjoyable. Judging by the way this business is growing, there is no shortage of customers who share my views.

An excellent book that promotes the concept of bringing some fun into the workplace is *Fish* by Stephen Lundin. The author bases his recommendations on his observations of a very successful fish mongering business at the Pike Place Fish Markets in Seattle. This book has sold millions of copies worldwide so there appears to be a lot of support for the idea that it is not only okay to bring some fun into your workplace, it is actually a very significant method to help build a successful business.

Lighten up your business and encourage your team to bring some humour and fun into the workplace. Personally I believe it shows the staff have a degree of confidence in the business when they feel comfortable enough to enjoy themselves.

What can you do today?

If you haven't already purchased a copy of the book *Fish*, today is the day. Buy it, read it and put some of the author's recommendations into action. If you already have a copy sitting on your bookshelf, open it up and pick out a few simple tips and action them.

#36 Encourage people to bring their personality to work

I believe that the days of the faceless employee are over and I say good riddance. Sterile workplaces, nameless faces and an overall sense of being just a number in the machine needed to go. People like personalities and I believe it is something that should be encouraged.

Sure, there is a limit—we can't have people being too over-the-top or gregarious to the point that it is intimidating, but encourage your staff to make work a reflection of themselves—it has many benefits. Most importantly your staff will enjoy their work a lot more. They will tend to be more relaxed and happier and they will feel a sense of ownership regarding the business. If they are enjoying themselves they will offer better levels of service and your customers will notice the difference.

How you encourage people to bring their personality to work is up to you. It might be personal items at their desk, it might be what they wear or what they say. Bringing personality into a business environment is being encouraged at senior management levels, in fact it is essential, so why not adopt the same principles at all levels of your business.

As a business owner and entrepreneur you bring your own personality and flair to work. Encourage others to do the same and your business will benefit from it.

What can you do today?

What is your philosophy towards your staff bringing their personalities to work? Is it something you have actually thought about? Why not sit down with your team and ask them their thoughts. Setting parameters can be a good idea, but as with any boundaries explain to your staff why they are in place.

#37 Beware of bad smells

Funnily enough some businesses really do stink—literally. A strange thought in the modern world where we have on offer about a million chemicals that can mask, destroy, enhance or modify just about any odour known to mankind. But it can be a problem.

In recent years there has been a lot of research done on how human senses affect buying patterns and decisions. Now we know that the visual side of a business is very important, but so are sounds and smells. Anyone walking past a hot chicken shop or a bakery knows the intoxicating effect these odours can have on the casual passerby, often leading them into the shop before they even know they are doing it.

If you work in the same place day in day out, you can start to become oblivious to bad odours. To you they are normal smells rather than offensive smells, but to your customers they may be a significant turn off. Again the human mind takes over and assimilates all of the information it receives. A dodgy smell creates the assumption that the business may be dodgy.

Equally as bad are those businesses where someone has discovered an oil burner and they are determined to stew lavender oil every minute of every day. Sure the smell may be nice occasionally, and in small doses, but it is very strong and overpowering. I stopped visiting one doctor's surgery because the smell of the essential oils burning was simply overpowering. With the standard 40-minute wait to see the doctor, my sense of smell was impaired for hours. So even though someone was trying to make the surgery more appealing they were actually doing more harm than good.

The very worst scenario is a food-based business that smells bad. Bad smells and food do not go well together in the same sentence, let alone in the same breath. Be aware of any bad or overpowering smells—they could be costing you business. Neutrality is the best path.

What can you do today?

Does your business stink? Hopefully not, but it might be worth doing the smell test and then addressing the issue to prevent possible loss of customers due to offensive or over-powering smells.

#38 Who is in control of the music?

Loud or inappropriate music in a business can turn customers away in droves. It is often a point overlooked or not given a lot of attention. Like all of the tips in this section, the aim is to make your business as appealing as possible to your customers. If the music is wrong or too loud, it isn't going to make your customers come in or stay and you will lose out.

I actively encourage people to bring their personality to work (see tip 36) but I am not sure this is appropriate when it comes to music—sorry. Have you ever sat in a restaurant with a friend and found it is impossible to carry on a conversation because the music is too loud? Have you ever walked into a shop only to leave a few minutes later because you're not into the latest Megadeth hit? Sure we all have our own musical tastes and one person's Beethoven is another person's Sex Pistols, but the important point here is to figure out what is appropriate for your customers, not your staff.

Just like smells, sounds have a lot of associated psychology. Research shows that some music does have an impact on a shopper's buying habits. In restaurants the faster the beat of the music the faster people tend to eat. So if you run a restaurant that focuses on high turnover with diners not spending a lot of time in the restaurant, music with a fast beat is appropriate. If you are running a fine dining establishment where patrons have the table for the night, it is preferable they take their time and hopefully purchase more food and beverages in doing so.

The same applies for music over the telephone system. The only thing worse than being on hold for five minutes with no music is being on hold for ten minutes with deafening music that forces you to hold the handpiece at arm's length.

The message here is to be aware of music and the role it plays in your business. Make it appropriate for your particular customers and make one person responsible for the music. This person needs to be given the appropriate guidelines for what to play and how loud it should be. They then make sure it happens.

What can you do today?

Think about the role music plays in your business. If you can incorporate it that is great, but assign one person to be in charge of the music according to very clear guidelines. Then let the rest of your team know and understand the importance of music and what is appropriate and what is not.

#39 Cleanliness is a key component to profitability

In tip 37 I spoke about the power of smells to have an impact on your business. Well, cleanliness can be a related issue but generally it deserves its own attention. I am amazed at the number of businesses that are downright filthy. Recently I had to purchase a set of tyres for my car and I had to wait while they were being fitted. Let me describe the waiting room.

There were two couches, covered in grime and grit where the workers sat during their breaks. There was a coffee table filled with really old, ragged magazines, all revealing various forms of semi-naked ladies promoting things to do with cars. There was a collection of cracked and broken cups with baked-in residue that had to be pre-World War I. There was coffee and sugar everywhere and a television playing static. To top it off, there was an overflowing ashtray that probably hadn't been emptied since people started smoking. Now I was the first customer in this business on that day and I was greeted with this sight. If I knew I had to wait in a tip I wouldn't have gone there and I certainly won't be going back. I see no excuse for this kind of mess, which is wrong in so many ways that I could write a book about it.

I stopped visiting a local coffee shop simply because it was always filthy. The tables were always covered in used cups and plates and as its seating was outdoors, the wind blew everything around. Added to this was the local pigeon population, which had figured out that this was an excellent foraging ground for leftover morsels. So in amongst the refuse was the added delight of pigeon droppings. All in all a very attractive place to stop for a coffee and piece of cake—not. To top it off, there were often four or five staff standing behind the counter waiting for a customer to turn up rather than going outside to clean up the mess. This was clearly just a poorly run business and one that has since cleaned up its act, I must say, but I am still emotionally scarred and hesitant to go there. I certainly would not order food from this business—if they could let the front of the business get so filthy what is the kitchen like?

Many retail shops and even offices are really dirty and grubby and there is no excuse for that. Customers expect, and I believe they are entitled, to visit a clean business. One area where a lot of businesses really lose customers is their toilets. Sure, keeping public toilets clean can be tough, but filthy toilets are a very big turn off for many consumers—they will go to a business where they know the toilets are clean, even if the products or services being sold are not as good.

A business that is not clean shows a lack of respect for itself, its customers and its staff. Successful businesses rarely have this problem.

What can you do today?

How clean is your business? Have a walk around and make a list of ten things you could do today to make your business cleaner and more appealing to everyone who deals with you.

#40 Make one person the keeper of the workplace

Often the hardest part about making your workplace truly winning is that there is no one person charged with this responsibility. I strongly recommend you make one person the 'keeper of the workplace' and their responsibility is to make sure the business always looks, sounds and smells its best.

If you are going to give this person that kind of responsibility (and for those single-person businesses I guess it's up to you) they will need to know exactly what is expected of them and most importantly why it is expected. Often these kinds of expectations can be seen as the semi-neurotic ramblings of an unreasonable business owner rather than the significant business essentials that they are. I believe the person in charge of keeping the workplace perfect plays one of the most essential roles within an organisation and it is important they are made aware of it.

Even though one person is committed to being in charge, everyone needs to work together to keep the business in the right outward shape. This is a trap that can easily snare the unwary. The other members of the team start to think it's not their responsibility so they stop washing cups or cleaning up after themselves. They can walk past rubbish on the floor and dismiss bad smells as someone else's problem, not theirs. So the keeper of the workplace will still need some support from the powers that be to make sure they aren't left to carry the entire workload.

What can you do today?

Assign your own keeper of the workplace and make sure you let everyone else know they have to pull their weight as well.

Action pages

Things I need to do to make my business more successful.
31 Have pride in your workplace (even if you are the only one there)
Action required right now

....
....
....
....

Completed (date, time and by whom)

....
....

32 Make your workplace inviting and easy for your customers to visit
Action required right now

....
....
....
....

Completed (date, time and by whom)

....
....

33 Don't scrimp on the little things (out with *Women's Weekly* 1972)
Action required right now

....
....
....
....

Completed (date, time and by whom)

....

....

34 Offer really good coffee and tea (and nice cups)
Action required right now

....

....

....

....

Completed (date, time and by whom)

....

....

35 Just add laughter (in vast amounts and often)
Action required right now

....

....

....

....

Completed (date, time and by whom)

....

....

36 Encourage people to bring their personality to work
Action required right now

....

....

....

....

....

Completed (date, time and by whom)

....

....

37 Beware of bad smells
Action required right now

....

....

....

....

Completed (date, time and by whom)

....

....

38 Who is in control of the music?
Action required right now

....

....

....

....

Completed (date, time and by whom)

....

....

39 Cleanliness is a key component to profitability
Action required right now

....

....

....

....

....

Completed (date, time and by whom)

. . . .

. . . .

40 Make one person the keeper of the workplace
Action required right now

. . . .

. . . .

. . . .

. . . .

Completed (date, time and by whom)

. . . .

. . . .

Brainstorming page

Use this page to write notes, comments, ideas or things to do regarding the preceding section. The aim is to improve your business a little every day, to make it more successful and for you to enjoy being an entrepreneur.

*'Enthusiasm is one of the most powerful engineers of success.
When you do a thing, do it with all your might.
Put your whole soul into it. Stamp it with your own personality.
Be active, be energetic, be enthusiastic and faithful,
and you will accomplish your object.
Nothing great was ever achieved without enthusiasm.'*

Ralph Waldo Emerson

6 | Marketing on a tight budget

Very few businesses have unlimited funds when it comes to marketing and, naturally, the opposite is more often the case: the business needs to do a lot of marketing on a tight budget. This is not a problem but the key to success when it comes to low-cost marketing is that it will involve effort rather than expenditure. This section looks at the key principles behind low-cost marketing and it makes some suggestions on how you can apply this principle to virtually any business.

\# 41   You have to stand out from the crowd
\# 42   If your budget is small you need to put in some elbow grease
\# 43   Ask people to send you business and they will
\# 44   Networking is not a dirty word
\# 45   Always be prepared for an opportunity
\# 46   Give away products or services to promote your business
\# 47   You need to commit time to marketing
\# 48   The Internet is here to stay—and it is amazing
\# 49   The power of the testimonial
\# 50   Do less but do it well

#41 You have to stand out from the crowd

Before you can even think about marketing your business you need to be committed to making your business stand out from the crowd. But what does this really mean? It means that every part of your business has to be better than your competitors. The way the business looks, the service you offer, the products or services you sell, your staff, your corporate image—the lot.

I have spoken about the threat of ever-increasing competition and how it impacts all businesses around the world. It is here to stay and it will keep increasing. For a business to truly succeed it needs to be better than its competitors in every way and this requires commitment and dedication from everyone involved in the business.

All of the recommendations put forward in this book highlight how to stand out from the crowd in a host of areas but unless that commitment is in place, nothing else will really get off the ground. A lot of businesses set out with the goal of being average and they achieve it perfectly. But the real gems, or the winning ones, know they want to be better than everyone else and they set out with this goal very clearly established.

What if your business has been operating for a while—and you are finding yourself being swamped by competitors that are bigger and bolder? I really don't think it matters and I certainly don't think that size has a lot to do with it. You can change your business philosophy today and start making the changes that are required to really make your business stand out from the crowd.

What can you do today?

Make the commitment right now that you want to make your business the very best it can be. Accept nothing less and you will achieve your goal.

#42 If your budget is small you need to put in some elbow grease

I often encounter business owners who have the perception that building a successful business requires a lot of money. From my own experiences and observations this is not necessarily true. There are countless examples of businesses that have had big cash injections to get started and they failed, miserably. Likewise there are countless examples of businesses that started on a shoestring and ended up as huge corporations. Money can help but it is by no means the be-all and end-all when it comes to building a successful business, and this is particularly relevant when you talk marketing.

The simple reality is that if you haven't got a big budget to spend on marketing your business, you need to be prepared to roll up your sleeves and do some hard work yourself. It's easy to spend a lot of money on advertising. Full-page ads in newspapers, on television and radio and most other forms of high-profile advertising will certainly get the phone ringing or the customers coming in the door, but it costs a lot of money. Often the return is nowhere near what you expect.

Low-cost marketing means you have to look for ways to market and promote yourself that generally require effort rather than budget. I have a client who does makeovers on balconies and courtyards and any other small spaces. She had a limited budget but enough money to have some nice brochures printed, which explained exactly what she did. My advice to her was to hit the pavements and put her brochures in the letterbox of every unit or apartment block in town and to her credit that is exactly what she did. Today she has built a very successful business from being prepared to put in that elbow grease.

There are literally too many examples of ways to market a business for very little money. The best piece of advice I can give is to buy a book that specialises on this topic. My first book was *101 Ways to Market your Business* and it is full of ideas and recommendations that fit into this category. There are also lots of others and they all generally contain great recommendations and tips that will cost very little money.

The aim of this tip is to get you thinking about low-cost marketing ideas and accept the fact that to make them happen the biggest requirement will be someone's time and effort.

What can you do today?

Pop down to your local bookstore and buy a book on low-cost marketing ideas. If you are not sure which one to buy, talk to other people in your network and you will find someone who will make a good recommendation. Buying the book is only the start, though. Putting the recommendations into place is the real key—commit to implementing one idea every day.

#43 Ask people to send you business and they will

Often one of the greatest sources of new business comes from referrals. Winning businesses tend to get more than their fair share of referrals from happy customers and this is a pretty good indication that what they are doing, they are doing well.

Surprisingly though, many of us often forget to ask our customers to refer business to us. Sometimes they need to be reminded. If you have happy customers (and I certainly hope you do), take a few minutes to ask them to tell their family, friends and workmates about you. Often people simply overlook referring business because they don't think to do it. But if you ask them to do it they will go out of their way.

The end result can often be that you build this wonderful network of people, all spreading the word about how wonderful your business is. Now imagine how much your business will grow if every customer you have today recommends you to just one other person. Potentially your business could double overnight.

How do you ask your customers to refer your business? There are a couple of options and it really depends on the type of business you run. A consulting firm might simply make it a closing statement at the end of the project: 'Thank you for your business and please tell your associates about the work we do'. It may be more formal, by mail, or a sign on the wall that says, 'If you are happy with what we do please tell your friends'. Unfortunately most of us are a little hesitant to ask for business and it really is something that needs to be overcome.

I recently gave advice to a clothing retailer about asking for referrals from their existing customers. I suggested they take the approach of talking to their customers and saying that they are looking to grow the business by attracting more customers. This meant their buying power would be greater so their existing customers would get even better value for money as prices might drop. This strategy worked well because not only did the existing customers take on the sales responsibility, they also had an incentive to promote the business. Everyone wins.

Winning businesses are built on word of mouth and it costs nothing. But you only get it if you deserve it.

What can you do today?

Think of a way to provide an incentive to get your customers to refer business to you and then get them working as your unpaid sales team.

#44 Networking is not a dirty word

Networking is a buzz word we all hear all of the time. Unfortunately for many business owners it evokes powerful images of standing around a room with a lot of people you don't know, feeling awkward and unsure. Networking is really just an excellent way to build a business. It's cheap, it's instant and it doesn't require a lot of exceptional skills.

Networking is about communication. Feeling awkward when meeting new people can be challenging but there are many simple techniques to make it easier. I learned a lot of my communication skills from a book I read at least once a year, *How to Win Friends and Influence People* by Dale Carnegie. The title sounds terribly manipulative but it really isn't. It is a book about communicating and the lessons learnt from those pages can be used time and time again, every day of the week. The end result will be that you will become a better communicator and you will find networking much easier.

The next part of the process is to go to a networking function with a clear goal. Your aim here is to meet people who might be potential customers or who might be able to refer business to you. Consider a few things ahead of time. Think about how you will introduce yourself and what you sell. If you meet someone who could become a customer or business associate how will you arrange to follow up? How will you end the conversation so that you can move on and meet other people without offending the person you are talking to? I know some entrepreneurial types who sit down and write a networking plan before they go to these functions, and they get excellent results. It is a business opportunity, not a social event, and they treat it as such.

Networking is here to stay. The better you are at it the more business you can attract. Go into any networking situation with an open mind and with a plan of attack.

What can you do today?

There are two things: the first is to buy a copy of *How to Win Friends and Influence People*. It will give you some excellent ideas on dealing with people and if you apply them your networking will become much easier. The next thing you can do right now is plan your next networking opportunity. Think about how you will introduce yourself, what questions you will ask the people you meet, how you will excuse yourself when it is time to move on and meet someone else. By simply being prepared you will find that networking can change from a chore to an enjoyable and rewarding experience.

#45 Always be prepared for an opportunity

The potential for a new customer is always just around the corner and the astute business owner and entrepreneur knows this fact well. They are always ready for action. To truly take advantage of any opportunity you need to be prepared. You need to keep a supply of business cards on you and your promotional material handy and be ready to talk to someone about what you do.

A common theme promoted in this book is that many business owners are outwardly shy when it comes to talking about their business. They are almost afraid of saying what they do. While the humility is nice, it really isn't a good strategy for building a business.

Look for any opportunity to promote your business and you will find plenty of them. Look at any chance encounter as an opportunity—who knows what will come out of it. I have made a surprising number of excellent contacts and customers from people I have sat next to on planes, or been forced to wait with in a queue, or just bumped into for some reason. If you are genuinely interested in other people, you will find they will reciprocate and be interested in you.

I am not advocating you stalk people, just that you be prepared to tell people about your business and be prepared to give them more information—never judge a book by its cover. I have come across a lot of people who at first glance may look more like they need a job rather than being in a position to give me work and it is easy to judge based on appearances alone. But by keeping an open mind you will not categorise people as quickly and the potential for a new customer could be standing right in front of you.

Interestingly, the starting point here is being able to say what it is you do. A lot of people actually struggle with this part of the interaction. When asked what they do there is a kind of mumble with downcast eyes. I recommend you have a very clear line in your mind: when asked what you do, stop, look the person in the eye and tell them loudly and proudly.

What can you do today?

Are you prepared for any opportunity? Do you keep business cards and promotional material readily access-ible? When asked what you do, do you answer in a loud and proud manner or do you mumble and look away? Today is the day to end bad habits and improve on good ones.

#46 Give away products or services to promote your business

This is the 'put your money where your mouth is' principle. While it might not work for all businesses it will work for most. If what you sell is as good as you say it is, be prepared to give potential customers a free trial or taste.

I recently worked on a marketing campaign with a health studio. They wanted to promote personal training as it was a good source of revenue for the business. At the end of the day we could have advertised special introductory offers to get the people in the doors but it was agreed that the best way to sell the service was to actually give potential customers a free personal training session. Now this was a big expense for the business but they felt their service and the overall personal training they offered was the best available, so they put their money where their mouth was. It paid off incredibly well. They promoted personal training sessions to their existing members as well as to the general public and they literally doubled their number of personal training clients in a very short amount of time.

This no risk, no commitment trial is a good option for customers. They can try a product or business without obligation and it is up to the business to sell themselves. If they don't measure up, the customer can walk away.

I often recommend to my clients to try this technique when looking for ways to build up their business and I have seen it work very successfully in businesses as diverse as restaurants, dance academies, training organisations, bakeries, filtered water suppliers, cleaning product manufacturers and professional service-based businesses. In my own business I offer a one-hour free consultation. This provides potential clients with the opportunity to assess the advice offered by my firm. If they like what they hear they come back, if they don't we never see them again. Nine out of ten people come back and I put a lot of this high success rate down to the fact that the client has the opportunity to make their own mind up in a non-pressured way with a clear understanding of what my business can offer them.

If you think your business is as good as it can be, try embracing the concept of a free trial or free product and enjoy the results. Analyse what it will cost you to make this offer and monitor the results. You may be pleasantly surprised.

What can you do today?

Can you offer a free product or service as a trial to potential customers? Why not trial it with a few potential customers and see how it works before you mass market the idea? You may want to keep this option as a clincher when it comes to closing a deal.

#47 You need to commit time to marketing

I mentioned at the beginning of this section that if you haven't got a lot of money to spend on marketing you need to commit your time to it. One of the biggest reasons for businesses failing to market themselves is that they don't allocate enough time to the process.

Successful businesses are normally good marketers. They know it is important and they make sure they devote the time necessary to market their business regularly. This is the key to their success, not the amount they spend.

Marketing needs to become as important as opening the doors in the morning. It needs the same attention as paying your bills or collecting money from your customers because it determines the long-term success of your business. But because it is less tangible and generally less demanding (if you don't do your marketing no one rings and chases you) it is easy to put off for another day. Another factor is the average business owner doesn't really know how to market. They are good at what they do but not at marketing, which is logical.

You can learn how to market. You can use your network of business associates and mentors to learn. If you ask people they will normally be very forthcoming in telling you what works for them. There are plenty of good courses that offer simple marketing skills for all levels of business experience, or else you can pay for a marketing consultant to teach you. Regardless of how you improve your skills, the point is you need to commit time to marketing.

In your diary and weekly schedule, there should be blocks of time marked out for when you focus on nothing but marketing your business. How much time that is is up to you. The more time you spend marketing the greater the results will tend to be but if you spend all of your time marketing and no time running your business the end result could be lots of new customers who leave because the business is poorly run.

Clearly it depends on the size of your business and your support staff.

What can you do today?

Go through your diary and block out time for the next week, and for all the weeks after when you can spend time on marketing your business. It *must* be adhered to. If you are not sure where to start, read a book that tells you how to market. Set up your files so that all of your material is at your fingertips. Meet with your business associates and mentors to get their advice and recommendations, but start it today.

#48 The Internet is here to stay—and it is amazing

I am a big believer in the power of the Internet. As a marketing tool it is unequalled in many ways. It is cost effective, it is convenient for customers to use, there are plenty of companies that can help you take advantage of it and it is used by more potential customers every day. The role the Internet plays in our everyday lives just keeps increasing. Ten years ago the thought of being able to pay all of your bills from your computer would have been a dream, now it is as normal as watching television. There is nothing that cannot be purchased over the net and businesses are becoming more and more creative about how to use the Internet to grow their business.

From a marketing point of view the Internet provides a very accessible way for customers to find out more about your business. They can do this at a time that suits them and without the added pressure of facing a salesperson. They can form an opinion of your business in the privacy of their own home, and this is exactly what they do.

Customers will use the net to research businesses. They will use it to find out more about the businesses that can provide whatever product or service they require. If your business is not online and your competitors are, they have a distinct advantage.

Having a good website is the bare minimum for any business. It should be professionally designed, visually impressive and easy to use. Design your website from a customer's perspective: what information would they like to see and how would they need to navigate the site? If you need to have lots of information arrange it in a way that doesn't make the site overly complicated or filled with page after page of information. Have easy-to-download information in pdf format so the format of the information doesn't change when it is printed out. Include pictures of you and your business—but optimise them so that the site loads quickly; remember we are all short of time and there is nothing more frustrating than waiting for what seems like an eternity for a website to load.

I still encounter people who think the Internet is a waste of time. No matter how much I try to convince them otherwise they have formed their opinion and it is unlikely to change. Generally these people don't use the net a lot themselves or they have a bad website that doesn't really work. They formulate their opinion based on the lack of traffic flow to their site. Having the site is the start, driving traffic to it is the next part. A web development company can advise you on how to increase traffic and this topic is a whole book in its own right. The fact is, though, it can be done and it isn't necessarily complicated or expensive.

Successful businesses accept and embrace the Internet as part of their overall marketing strategy.

What can you do today?

If you don't have a website, get the wheels in motion to make one happen today. Get a website designed and built to your budget—if you can only afford a one-page site, fine; grow it over time as you can afford it. If you do have a website, talk to your developer about how you can make it better and increase traffic flow. Websites are 'works in progress' that will never be finished, rather they are constantly evolving.

#49 The power of the testimonial

Testimonials are used to build credibility and they need to be a part of any marketing material you produce. Basically they are endorsements of your business from satisfied customers. Large companies use them all the time, most noticeably with high-profile celebrities endorsing their products and services. There is no reason why small businesses can't use testimonials just as effectively.

Testimonials help potential customers to make up their mind about using a new business because they are going by the recommendation of a third person. All businesses will tell you how great they are but to have an independent customer sharing their experience is far more convincing.

Collecting testimonials is easy (assuming you have plenty of happy customers). Every business should have a number of customers who are loyal and they are normally more than happy to offer a comment about your business. Asking for a written testimonial is fine; if they haven't got the time to write something down get them to do a verbal testimonial and copy it down.

Make absolutely certain though that the customer is happy for you to use their testimonial in marketing material. It is a little rude to assume that this is okay as some people may take offence if they are not asked. I like to actually get them to sign a release simply stating that the testimonial given is okay to be used.

The types of comments you are after are the ones that will state how satisfied the customer is with your business, products or services. Testimonials are recommendations so they are even more powerful if the customer states how long they have been using the business, why they use it and the fact that they intend to keep using it. This all helps to reinforce the message that your business, product or service is good.

Collecting testimonials can be time consuming and unfortunately most of us wait until we need them before collecting them. This makes the whole process a bit of a rush and often it gets forgotten or is put in the too hard basket. I recommend you collect testimonials on a regular basis and keep them in a folder. That way, as soon as you need them they are at your fingertips ready to be used.

Testimonials can be printed on brochures, listed on your website, hung on the wall of your business or used in your advertising.

What can you do today?

Start collecting testimonials today. Build up a supply that you can use in all of your promotional material. Once you have them make sure you use them—everywhere.

#50 Do less but do it well

When it comes to marketing there is a lot of value in the statement that it is better to do less but do what you do well. Rather than trying to action fifty great marketing ideas poorly, implement ten exceptionally well. These ten ideas then form a very solid and dependable core to your business' marketing activity. Further to this, it is much easier to monitor what is working and what is not and this is important when it comes to marketing. After all, what is the point of doing marketing if it doesn't work.

Like any business-related activity the dreaded FTI (failure to implement) is always lurking close by. If your 'to do' list is too long, it is more likely you won't get anything done which, as discussed previously, can have serious ramifications for your business.

The marketing process has more steps in it than most people realise. Each is equally important and it is easy to see that trying to do lots is not going to be as effective as taking a more strategic view to the entire process. The following list is a good guideline to understanding the steps involved in the marketing process from the beginning.

- Do your homework on your potential customers—who exactly do you want to do business with?
- Find out about your competitors—what they are offering—and determine what makes your business different.
- Establish your goals and objectives and be very clear about them.
- Get your product right.
- Develop your corporate image.
- Develop your promotional material.
- Determine how you will market to your targeted customers.

- Start implementing your marketing.
- Monitor and evaluate what you are doing.
- Keep marketing.
- Take a more controlled approach to your marketing—aim to do less but do it well and your business will enjoy greater results.

What can you do today?

What is your philosophy towards marketing? Are you trying to do lots without actually doing what you do well? Address each of the steps in the marketing process and identify which areas you need to improve to add more impact to your marketing.

Action pages

Things I need to do to make my business more successful.
41 You have to stand out from the crowd
Action required right now

. . . .

. . . .

. . . .

. . . .

Completed (date, time and by whom)

. . . .

. . . .

42 If your budget is small you need to put in some elbow grease
Action required right now

. . . .

. . . .

. . . .

. . . .

Completed (date, time and by whom)

. . . .

. . . .

43 Ask people to send you business and they will
Action required right now

. . . .

. . . .

. . . .

. . . .

. . . .

Completed (date, time and by whom)

....

....

44 Networking is not a dirty word
Action required right now

....

....

....

....

Completed (date, time and by whom)

....

....

45 Always be prepared for an opportunity
Action required right now

....

....

....

....

Completed (date, time and by whom)

....

....

46 Give away products or services to promote your business
Action required right now

....

....

....

....

....

Completed (date, time and by whom)

....
....

47 You need to commit time to marketing
Action required right now

....
....
....
....

Completed (date, time and by whom)

....
....

48 The Internet is here to stay—and it is amazing
Action required right now

....
....
....
....

Completed (date, time and by whom)

....
....

49 The power of the testimonial
Action required right now

....
....
....
....
....

Completed (date, time and by whom)

. . . .

. . . .

50 Do less but do it well
Action required right now

. . . .

. . . .

. . . .

. . . .

Completed (date, time and by whom)

. . . .

. . . .

Brainstorming page

Use this page to write notes, comments, ideas or things to do regarding the preceding section. The aim is to improve your business a little every day, to make it more successful and for you to enjoy being an entrepreneur.

'The greatest danger for most of us is
not that our aim is too high and we miss it,
but that it is too low and we reach it.'

Michelangelo

7 | If your business can't sell how can you succeed?

The whole reason any of us are in business is to sell something. Yet often this seems to be overlooked. Business owners build magnificent looking businesses and promote them extensively but when you finally pick up the phone or go into the business, their selling skills and abilities are terrible. You walk out in disgust. I am in no way advocating the hard sell or the pressure sell. Good selling skills are simply good customer service. People expect the person answering the phone or standing behind the counter to be able to meet their needs or at least point them in the direction of someone who can. Lousy selling skills are rampant in modern business, generally because of a lack of commitment from business owners to train staff due to the expense. Of course this is crazy, because the better your staff sell the more profitable the business will become.

\# 51   Do you really know what you are selling?
\# 52   Why should someone buy what you are selling?
\# 53   To be good at selling you have to be good at listening
\# 54   Get someone in to teach your staff how to sell—regularly
\# 55   Do you make it easy for people to buy from you?
\# 56   How you sold yesterday may not apply to how you sell today or tomorrow
\# 57   Become a sales analyser—every time you put your hand in your pocket

58   How do you monitor your sales?
59   What is the customer's main concern in the sales process?
60   Always ask for the sale

#51 Do you really know what you are selling?

I recently conducted a sales training seminar for a group of people in a telecommunications company. When I started to talk about product knowledge it soon became apparent that everyone in the group had different knowledge regarding the various products offered by the business and a lot of the information was conflicting. We had to stop and address each product and get the facts. A lack of product knowledge is a common problem and it is extremely frustrating for customers.

The reason for this lack of product knowledge and a general lack of sales skills is simply that a lot of people end up in sales rather than follow a set course to get there. One day they find themselves in a sales role and they simply do the best they can.

To make sure everyone involved in selling within your business is up to speed there has to be a very good level of communication. Time has to be spent talking about the products and services offered and this needs to be done regularly. Business runs at a pretty hectic pace these days and there is a mass of information available which often makes it hard to rummage through to find the facts among the hype.

Once you have product knowledge you need to be able to make a recommendation. This is another step in the sales process where many salespeople struggle. They can't make a recommendation based on what the customer is asking for— all they can do is give the customer options.

Do whatever it takes to make sure your staff are as knowledgeable as possible about the products and services you sell and your business will definitely stand out from the competition. If you need help why not get your suppliers to do presentations about the products that you sell.

What can you do today?

What steps can you take to make sure you and your staff have the best level of product knowledge for everything you sell in your business? Implement one activity today that will get the process moving.

#52 Why should someone buy what you are selling?

This is a good question and one that needs to be answered by anyone involved in selling for your business. Why should a customer buy from you? It is an interesting question and one I always ask when I am running a sales training programme.

Apart from product knowledge related questions it is often the hardest question to answer. As an exercise ask anyone in your business who is in a selling role why they think a customer should buy from them. The range of answers will probably be eye-opening.

This question requires an answer developed by all of your staff. Have a meeting and work through it until you can come up with the definitive statement. And it needs to be convincing—big and bold, not wishy washy and lukewarm.

Once you have a statement it needs to be introduced into every sales pitch, even if the customer doesn't ask the question. The customer will be thinking it so why not take control of the situation and let them know. It can be introduced by a statement such as, 'And you are probably wondering why you should buy this from us, not a competitor—well the answer is ....'

The reason why someone should buy what you are selling may change over time. It is a concept that needs to be revisited on a regular basis and it should be freely discussed. Try different versions of the definitive statement you have created. Does it close the deal or does the customer walk out when you say it? If they do, what you are saying is not convincing enough and it is time to go back to the drawing board.

What can you do today?

Have you got your definitive, 'Why should you buy from this business' statement? If not, today is the day to develop it. Get your staff involved and be prepared to talk about this concept a lot. When it stops working change it.

#53 To be good at selling you have to be good at listening

Ironically many salespeople miss the point when it comes to selling. They feel that to be a good salesperson you have to talk a lot and you need to talk fast. I think it is safe to say we are all over this kind of approach to selling.

To be truly good at selling you have to be good at two things. Firstly you have to be good at asking questions. But most importantly, you have to be very good at listening to the answers the customer gives.

We have all experienced quality sales service—you get asked intelligent questions and are then informed about your options based on the information you have given. Ideally you are then recommended a particular product or service. Perfect and really not that complicated. The 'normal' sales approach is to maybe ask you a token, parrot-like question, ignore your answer and then go into a sales speech based on what the salesperson wants to sell, not what you, the customer, wants to buy.

Listening is easier said than done. For a lot of people nerves make them talk a lot. Meeting a customer can be intimidating so they compensate by talking too fast and too much. Take a breath and get the customer to do the talking and you will be well and truly on the way to better sales performance.

If your salespeople are not good listeners, your business may be doomed to stay in the realms of mediocrity.

What can you do today?

Think about how you and your staff sell. Be a fly on the wall. Do you make the same mistakes as most salespeople? If you do, try the new approach next time you serve a customer.

#54 Get someone in to teach your staff how to sell— regularly

If you want your staff to sell more—train them. Give them the necessary skills to be good at selling and they will not only sell more they will also enjoy their job a lot more. Even though selling is not an overly complicated process or set of skills it does have a certain daunting feel to it that can be intimidating for some people. If they know how to overcome these feelings everyone wins.

I used to sell encyclopaedias door-to-door. Now that was a job where if you didn't sell you didn't eat. Your selling skills had to be pretty sharp. We had a supervisor who sat down with our team at the beginning of every shift to go over our sales techniques and skills. It really did get you in the right frame of mind before being unleashed on the suburbs.

If your staff need training it is generally better to get in an expert, someone who teaches people to sell all the time. They will be able to iron out problems quickly. With a good sales trainer you should notice an improvement in your figures pretty much straight away.

How often you get the trainer in is up to you. They will normally be able to put a programme together that will get the results you expect. Sales are sales, regardless of the business you are in. The techniques are generally the same so, even if you think your business is different or unique, they can be applied appropriately.

Successful businesses realise that well-trained sales staff are essential to making and keeping the business profitable.

What can you do today?

Take control of the sales training for your staff today. Get out the Yellow Pages and find a good sales trainer or talk to your business associates or mentors to get a recommendation.

#55 Do you make it easy for people to buy from you?

This is another one of those tips that seems to be obvious but many businesses struggle with the concept. They have adopted overly complicated procedures that make buying anything a nightmare. They don't take credit cards, they are hard to get to, they don't have enough sales staff, you have to order products and wait weeks for them to arrive—all in all they just seem to miss the point.

If you want your business to develop a reputation for being magnificent, make it as easy as possible for your customers to buy your products. If you don't they will go to somewhere that does.

The key word here is 'simple'. Keep it simple, in every possible way. To do this you need to be a keen observer of how your sales system works. Is it streamlined? Is it set up to be convenient for you but not for your customers? Look at everything you do—all from a customer's perspective with the one overriding objective being ease of purchase.

I often hear business owners saying they don't take some credit cards because the merchant rates are too high. Put your prices up to cover the costs and accept the credit cards. Think about the last time you went to a business and they wouldn't accept the credit card you wanted to use. It was an inconvenience and an irritation. Your customers expect to use their preferred particular credit card and if you don't accept it they are likely to go elsewhere.

What difficulties have you encountered in the buying process and would you go back to the business where you were confronted with the problem?

What can you do today?

Look at your business and try to find one way to make it easier for your customers to buy from you. Often that is all it takes. If you don't take credit cards you really do need to. Ring your local bank and get the process in motion.

#56 How you sold yesterday may not apply to how you sell today or tomorrow

Customers are changing and their needs and expectations are changing constantly. How this affects customer service has been discussed in a previous section but it is worth discussing how it affects selling.

It is easy for a business to fall into the trap of creating a rigid sales process so that everyone who sells follows the same format. In fact this is generally a good process, but if the process is not reviewed on a regular basis you may start to lose customers. As the customers' needs and expectations change, the sales process you use will need to be modified.

Imagine how butchers had to change how they sold beef in the United Kingdom after the mad cow disease outbreak. It would have been different to the way they did it before. This is obviously an extreme example but look at how travel is sold these days. The words 'safe destination' are now well and truly implanted in the sales pitch for most holiday destinations, a concept we were aware of but not as an everyday accepted risk assessment for when we plan our holidays as it has become today.

The point I am trying to make is that we need to review how we sell our products and services on a regular basis. There is really no room for the old, 'That's the way we always did it' mentality. Sales are dynamic and ever changing, regardless of the business. It is the customers who drive sales and the more flexible and adaptable your business the greater your chances of succeeding where others fail.

What can you do today?

Today is the day to review your sales process to see if you have become a little set in your ways. If you have, turn it upside down and breathe some life into it.

#57 Become a sales analyser—every time you put your hand in your pocket

To become better at selling you need to become a better observer of how other businesses do it. Every time you make a purchase start reviewing the way you were sold. Look for the good and the bad. Take the good observations and, if you can, incorporate them into your own business.

Because we are so used to going into various businesses and making a purchase it is easy to go through the process on auto pilot. But if you start to become more observant it can be very interesting. You start to notice a lot more, you can sense when a sale is lost by the salesperson or when the sale is made. Standing in a queue can have some benefits—not many I might add—but it does give you time to watch what is happening.

I enjoy it a lot more when there is a good salesperson at work. It is interesting to see how they develop a rapport with the customer, ask the right questions, listen to the answers and respond accordingly.

When you do become an observer it helps if you are a little prepared. I talk about keeping a notebook on you elsewhere in this book and this is one of those situations when it will come in handy. As soon as you see something, good or bad, that strikes a chord make a note of it and refer to it later.

After a while you will collect a lot of valuable information that could be beneficial to your business.

What can you do today?

Next time you go into a business to buy something, observe how they handle the sale. Do they simply take your money or do they actually sell their products to you? Try to do this every time you buy something this week and you will be surprised at how much information you take in and the tips you pick up.

#58 How do you monitor your sales?

All businesses monitor the money coming in—it is the lifeblood of the business—and cash flow is one of those areas that always needs attention. But when it comes to monitoring sales, businesses generally pay less attention to detail.

If you sell only one product for a fixed amount it is pretty easy to figure out how many you sold at the end of the trading day. Few businesses, however, have this level of simplicity. You need to pay particular attention to what you are selling or, more importantly, what isn't selling and why.

Sales reports can be simple one-page documents kept beside the cash register to be filled in whenever a sale is made. Better than this is a clever cash register that breaks the sales down according to pre-determined categories. As long as your staff press the right keys the information should be pretty accurate.

Regardless of how you monitor your sales, the information collected needs to be reviewed and ideally compared to the last week, last month and even last year. This way you start to develop a greater feel for any sales trends that happen within your business. This is very valuable information as it allows you to develop a much more strategic approach to selling. Larger organisations (and also a lot of smaller ones) have very detailed sales reports. They know the value of understanding what is selling and what isn't within a business.

The bottom line is that the more control and understanding you have of the products and services you sell the more likely you are to develop a sustainable business. It takes the hit-and-miss factor out of the equation.

What can you do today?

How can you improve your sales monitoring process within your business? Is it time to upgrade your cash register or buy some new software to give you answers? If you don't have a system, put one in place today—start with a simple form beside your cash register.

#59 What is the customer's main concern in the sales process?

As a customer our biggest concerns when it comes to buying are whether the product we buy will not work as it should, whether we are paying too much for it or if it breaks we will have thrown our money away. It is all a brief psychological risk-assessment process that often happens without us even knowing it is happening. If you can dispel these concerns you will be well and truly on the way to increasing sales.

So, how do we do that? Let's look at the first one first—the product not working as it should. Clearly you need to tell the customer that if for any reason they are not satisfied with the way the product works they can bring it back and either exchange it or get a refund (depending on your policy). If there are conditions let them know in advance, don't make it a surprise.

If they are concerned about paying too much, explain your pricing policy and if you are more expensive than other places explain why. Perhaps you have better after-sales service. Maybe the products are slightly different. Or your business is smaller than the competitors and while you may not have the buying power you make up for it with more personalised service. Give the customer the facts and let them make their own decision. For long-term repeat business it is much better to be up front than to let the customer find out for themselves and feel ripped off.

Finally, explain how your guarantee system works. Be specific and make sure the customer is clear on the life of the guarantee and what it covers. If it doesn't have a guarantee, explain why. Some products don't and there is a legitimate reason for this. If you buy a goldfish and it dies you are unlikely to be able to get a refund.

By addressing the above in a few short sentences, the customer's concerns are alleviated and they should be happy to buy the product. When was the last time you had someone explain away your concerns in that manner? Probably not recently but if you do it in your business, you will soon be classified as one of the winning ones.

What can you do today?

What are you doing to remove concerns that your customers may have regarding buying your products? Think about how you will answer those concerns and make sure your staff can answer the customers' concerns accurately as well. Try it—you will be amazed at the results.

#60 Always ask for the sale

The last and most fatal sales mistake is quite simply not asking for the sale. This means being prepared to ask the customer for their business and it is often described as the point when most sales are lost. The salesperson can go through the whole process, but they simply don't ask for the business at the end.

What does 'ask for the sale' actually mean? It means asking the customer if they would like to buy the item you are selling and it really is that simple. This is that awkward moment when the customer is deciding if they want to make the purchase or not. If the salesperson is standing there waiting expectantly, often the customer will walk away from the sale simply because they feel under pressure to make a decision.

I have a lot of sales reps coming to my business to sell various products. I sit through presentation after presentation and then most of them just pack up and leave without even asking me if we can do business together.

By asking the customer if they would like to buy the product you are not being pushy—you are simply trying to help them to make a decision. Clearly it would be better for the business if they did buy the product but they can still say no at this stage.

Be prepared to ask for the sale.

What can you do today?

Do you and your staff ask for the sale? If not, why not? What is the barrier stopping this from happening? Is it a simple matter to correct? If you are not sure how to handle it, revert back to getting a professional sales trainer to come and help you work it out.

Action pages

Things I need to do to make my business more successful.
51 Do you really know what you are selling?
Action required right now

....
....
....
....

Completed (date, time and by whom)

....
....

52 Why should someone buy what you are selling?
Action required right now

....
....
....
....

Completed (date, time and by whom)

....
....
....

53 To be good at selling you have to be good at listening
Action required right now

....
....
....
....
....

Completed (date, time and by whom)

....
....

 # 54 Get someone in to teach your staff how to sell—regularly
Action required right now

....
....
....
....

Completed (date, time and by whom)

....
....

 # 55 Do you make it easy for people to buy from you?
Action required right now

....
....
....
....

Completed (date, time and by whom)

....
....

 # 56 How you sold yesterday may not apply to how you sell today or tomorrow
Action required right now

....
....
....
....

Completed (date, time and by whom)

....
....

57 Become a sales analyser—every time you put your hand
in your pocket
Action required right now

....
....
....
....

Completed (date, time and by whom)

....
....
....

58 How do you monitor your sales?
Action required right now

....
....
....
....

Completed (date, time and by whom)

....
....
....

59 What is the customer's main concern in the sales process?
Action required right now

....
....

....

....

Completed (date, time and by whom)

....

....

....

....

60 Always ask for the sale
Action required right now

....

....

....

....

Completed (date, time and by whom)

....

....

Brainstorming page

Use this page to write notes, comments, ideas or things to do regarding the preceding section. The aim is to improve your business a little every day, to make it more successful and for you to enjoy being an entrepreneur.

'If you don't ask, you don't get.'
Mahatma Gandhi

8 | Question everything— constantly

Having an open and inquisitive mind is probably the most powerful asset any budding entrepreneur can have. Business is not static these days, it is changing constantly, it is exciting, it is challenging and we all need to be striving to keep up and hopefully lead the way in this environment. To truly stand a chance at becoming successful you need to be able to honestly appraise what you are doing every day and look for ways to do it better. You can't sit back and be content that your business will be just as successful in the coming years as it has been in the past few years if you don't review and modify what you do. You need to question everything you do and you need to question it regularly. I love this about experienced entrepreneurs—they are not afraid to ask anyone for an opinion about what they do or for a suggestion to make their business better. In this section we are going to be looking at how to question everything you do.

61 Without this there is no point asking questions
62 Question your business partners—ask them to be honest
63 Walk around your business—and really look at everything
64 Go to successful businesses and find out why they are successful
65 Mystery shop your way to success
66 Do you charge enough?

67   If it doesn't feel right it probably isn't—the business owner's sixth sense

68   Talk to your staff—ask them for ideas and their opinions

69   Don't be afraid to be a manager—sometimes it's tough

70   Write your own operations manual as a way to question what you do

#61 Without this there is no point asking questions

This section covers the importance of being able to question and review everything you do in your business. If you are not prepared to accept what you find out or to do something about it, don't bother asking the question.

Many business owners are rigid and set in their ways. They think they want to hear about their business from their customers but what they want to hear is just the good stuff—they don't want to know about any negatives and, often, they can get quite hostile.

It is a real sign of business maturity to be able to take constructive criticism on board and use it to make your business even better. Think about it, how grateful would you be if someone's honesty gave you the opportunity to make your business better?

Businesses that operate as if they are set in stone are dinosaurs and many can't survive in the modern business environment where the need to change and evolve is here to stay. Ask lots of questions of the people you deal with on a regular basis. If you ask the questions, have an open mind about the answers. You have to make the final decision about what you will do with the information.

What can you do today?

Do you have an open mind to constructive criticism? How do you respond if someone tells you something not so flattering about your business? If you do have an open mind, great—ask more people for their opinions and recommendations and use the information wisely. If you don't, it's time to work on opening up and becoming more flexible. Think about constructive criticism or feedback about your business as an exceptional opportunity and be sincerely grateful to the people giving you this feedback.

#62 Question your business partners—ask them to be honest

In this instance I would consider business partners to mean anyone you have a relationship with—your professional advisers (lawyer, accountant), your suppliers, friends in business, your business mentors and really anyone else who is in a position to know about your business.

Just as we have discussed the importance of asking your customers for their feedback and their recommendations to improve your business, your business partners can offer excellent advice from a different perspective. An open-minded business owner has access to a lot of good information and advice from their network of business partners—all you have to do to access this network is to ask.

Look for ways to run your business better, for successful marketing ideas, for new products and services and for ways to attract more customers. Just one good idea from a business partner could be a significant turning point for your business but you have to be big enough to ask.

Often it can be interesting to see the different perspective your business partners bring to your business. They will have different views and ideas developed from being involved in their own industries and businesses and their opinions and ideas really may be things you would not have even considered.

Sitting down with a business partner and asking them how you could make your business better is a little tough and it puts them on the spot. I suggest making a small list of topics that might include things such as customer service, product range, sales, advertising, business appearance and so on. Use this list to guide the conversation. This also gives you an opportunity to write their responses. If you do this exercise with ten business partners you might start to see some common themes emerging.

Be prepared to ask your business partners for their ideas and recommendations. Most will give their honest opinions freely but, remember, if you ask for them be prepared to listen.

What can you do today?

Make up a list of the areas of your business that you would like to discuss and then pick one business partner per day for the next week to ask for their opinions and feedback on how you could make your business better.

#63 Walk around your business—and really look at everything

When you visit the same place every day, year after year, it is very easy to walk in and out with blinkers on. Throughout this book I have made the recommendation that you stop what you are doing and go and really look at certain aspects of your business—whether it is your front entrance, your signage, your staff, your customers, whatever. Well, this tip is really to reinforce that message.

You need to become more observant in your business. You need to not only look more closely at every aspect of your business but also to be able to make changes that will improve the business.

As a business grows it is easy for the owners to lose touch with a lot of the every day events going on. While it becomes impossible and in some ways unproductive for the business owner to know all of the nuts and bolts it is important for them to have a clear understanding of how things work. The more they understand the more they can look for ways to make things run better.

You need to get out of your work space and just walk around. Clear your head, open your eyes and try to look at the business without your normal blinkers on. Talk to your staff, talk to some customers. Go across the road and look at your business, have a good look at your website, read through your own brochure and look at the products that you have on display.

There are so many aspects of the business that need to be reviewed on a constant basis that it can be daunting. The first step is to remove the blinkers and open your mind to becoming an observer. After a week of doing this it will become second nature. The habit of walking in and out of your business with blinkers on has probably formed over many years.

Once you become a keen observer you can then start to make the business even better—and that can take it from mediocrity to magnificence.

What can you do today?

Stand up and take a walk around your business and really look at it. Often you will be amazed by the things you see that you hadn't noticed before. It is all about shifting your perceptions and opening the mind. The benefits for you will be that your business will improve by you paying attention to the smaller details.

#64 Go to successful businesses and find out why they are successful

This is good advice and again it is along the theme of becoming an excellent business observer. Whenever you find out about a really successful business—perhaps they have won an award or your family and friends are talking about them or there may have been an article in the newspaper—I suggest you pay the business a visit. What they sell really doesn't matter; how they run the business does. What makes it so successful? Why do people keep coming back? Why does it win awards?

So you need to go in armed (metaphorically speaking of course) to find out their secrets and to see if you can apply any of them to your business. Often finding out why a business does so well is not clearly obvious on first inspection. From my own experience, it is more the way they do business rather than any one specific detail. It is the attitude of the staff, it is the attention to detail and it is the inviting and welcoming feel of the business. Rarely is it their pricing, a misconception that many business owners are far too preoccupied with.

Becoming a good observer of anything takes time and training. A quick walk around a successful business might give you a few clues but you need to really go a little deeper. Give them a call and make an enquiry about their product. Consider how they handle it. Most importantly, after the call did you feel like going to this business? Take the time to get to know that business, listen to their sales staff, make a purchase and see how the transaction is handled, or ask a few difficult questions. Whatever you do, try to get a very good feeling for the business.

Make a list of what you feel makes this business so good at what it does and beside each of the points indicate if they could be applied to your business. Then set about implementing them.

What can you do today?

We all know about those businesses that seem to be considered the best at what they do (hopefully it's yours). Well, find one and pay it a visit. Go there with your observer's hat on and try to clearly identify what makes them so good at what they do. Can you apply the same ideas to your business and do them even better?

#65 Mystery shop your way to success

Mystery shoppers are used by more businesses every day to provide an independent evaluation of what the business is doing well and what it could be doing better. They are not witch hunts trying to find the underachieving employee who can then be thrown to the wolves. They are mechanisms for giving an honest appraisal of a business.

Companies that offer mystery shopping services can be found in most cities. Often this is a service provided by marketing companies and training organisations. In more recent times, firms that do nothing but offer customer service evaluations, utilising mystery shoppers as one of their key resources, are being set up.

Ideally no one, not even the business owner, will know when a mystery shopper will be dropping by. They will appear just like any other customer and that is the aim. A short while later a report will be issued and the overall performance of the business can be measured. Periodically the mystery shopper evaluation can be repeated to determine if the business has improved or worsened.

Normally the first mystery shopper is the tough one. It highlights the most glaring weaknesses and it can be quite confronting for the business owners and the staff. Often the initial response is to point the finger and blame, which is not the best course of action. What is needed following this first report is a clear and level-headed plan to rectify any problems and to work at improving the business in any of the areas that need improving.

Mystery shoppers can be used to evaluate the following:

- service and selling skills offered over the telephone
- how easy the business is to find
- how appealing the entrance is
- general layout of the business

- first impressions
- overall cleanliness of the business
- overall ambience of the business (smells, sounds etc.)
- appearance of the staff
- selling skills of the staff
- perceived value for money
- general level of customer service
- response time to internet enquiries
- quality of the products or services sold.

There are many other related and specific areas of any business that can be evaluated and the information is usually valuable. While it can be a little confronting the end result is that your business will have the opportunity to rectify problems that can be losing you customers.

It is also interesting to note that if your staff know you are having regular mystery shoppers they tend to try a little harder as they never quite know if the customer standing in front of them is today's mystery shopper. Because of this, it is important to share any mystery shopper findings, good and bad, with your staff. Show them the information that is collected and that you are doing something with it.

It takes a strong business to use mystery shoppers—but they are a great way to work out the difference between mediocre and winning.

What can you do today?

Can you use mystery shopper evaluations to build your business? If you can, why not arrange one today?

#66 Do you charge enough?

Pricing is a tough subject—do you charge too much or too little? There are a lot of businesses that simply don't charge enough, making it really difficult to ever make the business successful. I received some very good advice when I was starting out in my business life—a very successful friend and entrepreneur sat me down and said, 'Someone has to be the most expensive and it may as well be you. But if you are going to be the most expensive you have to be the best at what you do. Your business has to shine in every way.' An interesting concept and one I have tried to adhere to in any business I have run.

I believe customers are less concerned with pricing as they are with service and value for money. Sure there are a lot of businesses that operate in price conscious markets. But even in these markets I believe the same principle applies—people will pay more for quality.

If your business runs on tight margins it is hard to make it magnificent as so much energy has to be focused on just making ends meet. If you can gradually build your prices up with the aim being to offer better service and better experience to your customers, in general it will pay off.

Charging what you are worth is a hard concept for a lot of people. They charge what they think their customers are prepared to pay and often the two are a long way apart. If your business doesn't make enough money it will not be successful, simple as that. If you are just scraping by and not really getting ahead in your business, maybe you are simply not charging enough.

Winning businesses are not afraid to charge what they are worth because they can back it up by being the best at what they do.

What can you do today?

Today is a good day to review what you charge. Look at all of your pricing and see if you can charge more and deliver a better product and a higher level of service.

#67 If it doesn't feel right it probably isn't—the business owner's sixth sense

I have spoken about the business owner's sixth sense with a lot of entrepreneurs and I have experienced it myself many times. It is the ability to be able to tell intuitively that something is not right in your business, it is the ability to be able to sense that something is wrong with a proposed deal or the person sitting across the desk from you who is saying something you don't quite believe. It most certainly exists, and those aware of it use it to their advantage. They encourage this sixth sense to grow and they listen when it needs to be heard.

This sense develops over time and it is just as relevant in life as it is in business. We need to learn to listen to this little voice at the back of our mind. Any time I have ignored it, it has either cost me money or caused me grief.

This is one of those tips where I am sure some readers will assume I have lost the plot but I have no doubt many will know exactly what I am talking about. There are many intangible aspects of running a business that have as much impact and bearing on succeeding as the more tangible and real aspects.

Have you ever been in a situation in your business when it just doesn't feel right but you ignore the nagging feeling and go ahead anyway only to find out it was a bad decision? Well that tingling wasn't your spider sense, it was your business owner's sixth sense trying to get out and to be heard. It is a priceless tool that will help you as an entrepreneur to be far more successful and enjoy your business if you let it.

What can you do today?

From today try to listen to your business owner's sixth sense. When you have nagging doubts, try to decide whether it is just fear or natural caution, or more of a gut feeling. The more you listen to your sixth sense the more it will talk to you.

#68 Talk to your staff—ask them for ideas and their opinions

Many businesses take an almost us-and-them approach to their staff. For most of us, life without staff would be pretty hard. Our businesses would never be able to grow, our workloads would be enormous and there would be a hollow feeling when it comes to sharing the trials and tribulations experienced in our daily business life.

Involve your staff in your business. Ask them for their ideas and their opinions, after all, they often know your business almost as well if not better than you. Most certainly they will know the specific jobs they do better than you. The more you let your staff play an active role in your business the more they will grow, the more ideas they will come up with and ultimately the better your business will run and the more successful it will be.

Involving your staff means asking for their opinions and thoughts. It means taking these opinions and thoughts seriously and being appreciative of the fact that your staff members are prepared to be involved. Just because you give them a weekly pay packet doesn't mean they have to open up; it is a real trust situation and it needs to be well handled.

Just as I spoke previously about the importance of treating your customers with respect, I think you should have the same level of respect for your staff. Sure, there will always be times when you drive each other crazy or make mistakes but you are working on the same team.

Get your staff involved in your business. Ask them for their thoughts and opinions and build a strong relationship based on mutual respect.

What can you do today?

What is your attitude towards your staff? Is it us-and-them or have you got a team? Do you ask your staff for their input on running your business and do you take their advice seriously? Write a simple paragraph on your views about your relationship with your staff and how you would like to see it evolve.

#69 Don't be afraid to be a manager—sometimes it's tough

Being a manager is a big task. It covers an enormous amount of ground and it is constantly changing. Being a manager means being a leader, it means being a decision maker and it means being committed to what you do.

As a business owner you fall into the role of being a manager by default and sometimes that can be the hardest part of running your business. You know how to do your business but you may never have had to manage people before so it is a whole new ball game.

Being a manager sometimes means making tough decisions. Sometimes staff just don't work out and they have to be dismissed. You have to make decisions that affect the lives of others. There is a balance between what is best for the individual and what is best for the business. Remember that many people study for years to become business managers.

Having commitment to becoming a better manager starts in your own head. Sure you will make mistakes, but as long as you learn from them your skills will improve. Understanding and accepting the complexity of being a manager is one part, but realising you are not expected to know everything overnight is the real key to becoming a good manager.

Read books on management styles and ideas—there are an amazing number around. Do a management course and ask your mentors for their ideas and advice. You will become a better manager for it, which is very rewarding personally, and your business will benefit from your increased ability as a manager.

What can you do today?

If you are in a position where you need to be a manager, make a commitment today to be the best manager you can be. Enrol in a managerial course or buy a book about being a better manager. Treat it like learning any new skill.

#70 Write your own operations manual as a way to question what you do

An operations manual is simply a written description of how your business operates on a daily basis. You should have one, regardless of the size of the business. Operations manuals put details in black and white and writing one is the perfect way to question why you do things in a particular way.

An operations manual can be as complex or as simple as you want it to be. It is going to be used internally by other members of your team, not put on display for the general public to read. It should outline how any situation should be processed within your business; for example:

* the opening procedures for the business
* expectations regarding staff appearance and conduct
* customer service procedures
* processing sales
* handling complaints
* ordering stock
* paying accounts
* company policy on staff entitlements
* use of company vehicles
* cleaning within the business.

The list really is endless and clearly it depends on the type of business you run.

Writing a manual like this really does make you investigate every part of your business in a detailed manner. Having written a few and advised my clients to write them the same feedback comes out every time—writing an operations manual is a work in progress. As you start writing a section, you start thinking about how it works and come up with better ideas on the spot. So the end product is helpful for making sure everyone knows what to do within your business but the writing process is great for questioning what you do and coming up with ways to do things better.

What can you do today?

If you haven't got an operations manual, today is the day to start it. First, make a list of all of the operational aspects of your business and then start filling in the details. Accept the manual will be a work in progress. If you have an operations manual already, determine whether it is current and still accurate. Pull it out and read it cover to cover; I am sure you will make changes for the better.

Action pages

Things I need to do to make my business more successful.
61 Without this there is no point asking questions
Action required right now

....
....
....
....

Completed (date, time and by whom)

....
....

62 Question your business partners—ask them to be honest
Action required right now

....
....
....
....
....

Completed (date, time and by whom)

....
....

63 Walk around your business—and really look at everything
Action required right now

....
....
....
....
....

Completed (date, time and by whom)

....

....

64 Go to successful businesses and find out why they are successful
Action required right now

....

....

....

....

Completed (date, time and by whom)

....

....

65 Mystery shop your way to success
Action required right now

....

....

....

....

Completed (date, time and by whom)

....

....

66 Do you charge enough?
Action required right now

....

....

....

....

Completed (date, time and by whom)

....

....

 # 67 If it doesn't feel right it probably isn't—the business owner's sixth sense
Action required right now

....

....

....

....

Completed (date, time and by whom)

....

....

 # 68 Talk to your staff—ask them for ideas and their opinions
Action required right now

....

....

....

....

Completed (date, time and by whom)

....

....

 # 69 Don't be afraid to be a manager—sometimes it's tough
Action required right now

....

....

....

....

Completed (date, time and by whom)

. . . .

. . . .

 # 70 Write your own operations manual as a way to question what you do
Action required right now

. . . .

. . . .

. . . .

. . . .

Completed (date, time and by whom)

. . . .

. . . .

Brainstorming pages

Use these pages to write notes, comments, ideas or things to do regarding the preceding section. The aim is to improve your business a little every day, to make it more successful and for you to enjoy being an entrepreneur.

....

....

....

....

....

....

....

....

....

....

....

....

....

....

....

....

....

....

....

....

....

....

....

....
....
....
....
....
....
....
....
....
....
....
....
....
....
....
....
....
....
....
....
....
....
....
....
....
....
....
....
....

'The return we reap from generous actions is not always evident.'
Francesco Guicciardini

9 | Become the ultimate corporate citizen

As business owners and entrepreneurs we make our living from the community where we live and work. I believe very strongly that it is important to give as much back to your community as you can. This needs to be done in a sincere way; not in the anticipation of receiving accolades or acknowledgment. If you do get recognition, accept it with pride—it is okay to be told you have done something good. In my opinion, those businesses that are great corporate citizens deserve every success that comes their way. There are a multitude of ways in which a business can be a good corporate citizen and these are covered in this section.

71   Be involved in the community where you do business
72   Look for opportunities outside of the normal
73   Stand up and be counted
74   Share your knowledge and experience with others
75   Encourage your staff to be good corporate citizens
76   Some things can't be measured in dollars and cents
77   Invest in the future of your industry
78   Offer praise wherever possible to other members of the community
79   Don't be afraid to tell people you are a good corporate citizen
80   Make up a plan to make you the ultimate corporate citizen

#71 Be involved in the community where you do business

First and foremost we have to start at the beginning and that simply means getting involved. Every community has a host of organisations where people give their time freely to get behind good causes that need some help. They may be charities, they may be environmental groups, they may be groups trying to improve conditions for particular members of the community. The choice is up to you. If you have a particular passion, use it to get involved.

Who has the spare time to get involved in community-based groups? Generally none of us but typically the people I meet who are doing the most in their community are the busiest of all. They run their own businesses, manage their families, try to find time for themselves and yet they still get involved. Why? Because it makes them feel good.

If you can't find the time to get involved yourself, support community groups with the products or services your business offers. Donate money to them or let them use your facilities to help raise money.

I choose two or three special events to offer my firm's services free of charge every year. This means that at any one time we will have a project we are working on that is community based. I am happy to cover the cost of this and my staff get behind it as well. We all feel great and to be honest the events have a greater chance of succeeding if they have access to professional event management and fundraising advice.

Whatever level of involvement you can offer, embrace the community where you live and run your business and play an active role in making it a better place for everyone living there.

What can you do today?

How involved are you in your community? A lot or not at all? If you are involved a lot, you can sit this one out—you deserve the break. If you're not involved at all, today is the day to get involved. Talk to your staff about what you would like to do and ask for their suggestions on how you could get more involved in your community. It might be something as simple as sponsoring a junior sporting team or it may be ambitious, such as raising a pile of money to build a facility for disabled people.

#72 Look for opportunities outside of the normal

Trying to decide how to get involved in your community can be quite challenging as there are so many opportunities; however, there are always some opportunities that are a little less obvious but equally worthy.

A while back I used to work for a bus company operating specialised tours. One day I read in the paper the local blood bank was having trouble getting office workers to donate blood. A little research showed that the main cause was the time it took for the workers to leave the office, have some lunch, get to the blood bank, donate and then get back to work. It just took too long. So we offered to put on a special bus service where the workers could eat their lunch on the way to the blood bank. We guaranteed to have them back at work within an hour and in a short amount of time we had built up a regular following of donors.

The bus service was free and the blood bank had a noticeable increase in donations when the service was running.

What can you do today?

Look for problems in the community and see if you can offer a solution. It may not be as big and bold as some community-based projects but to the people involved it is equally as important. Plus it is a rewarding experience to be able to solve a problem yourself. Read the newspapers, listen to the news and look for problems where your business could help provide a solution.

#73 Stand up and be counted

When you get caught up in your own business it is easy to start to break your life into two very distinct halves—the business half and the non-business half. The business half can easily become the biggest part, after all you have a lot riding on it and you are enthused and passionate about what you do. While this is happening, you need to keep playing a role in the other areas of your life.

Business owners are generally respected in the community. People understand they give a lot back to the community, they provide jobs and they make the economy go round. For this reason their opinions are valued. This makes it very important for business owners to play an active role in the running of their community.

When there are important issues being debated in your community have your say. Voice your opinion and don't be afraid to be a little controversial. It is easy to say nothing in case you might offend a customer who has a different opinion but it is more important to stand up for injustice or the things within your community worth fighting for.

When you have your own business don't stop being a part of the community where you live. Write a letter, voice an opinion, call the local radio station—whatever it takes just play a role.

What can you do today?

Have you become an observer of your community or do you play an active role? If it's been a while since you were able to get passionate about things you disagree with in your community maybe today is the day to redirect some of your business passion back into the place you call home.

#74 Share your knowledge and experience with others

Helping other businesses to grow and succeed is a worthy community activity. You can offer to share your experiences at a business gathering or even a presentation at a school. It is surprising how many of these organisations struggle to find interesting people to share their knowledge and experiences.

Take on a work experience student in your office. Give them the opportunity to see if they like the industry you are in. Think back to when you did something similar and how you found it benefited you. But don't wait for the schools to contact you, give them a call yourself and let them know you are interested in taking on work experience students.

Coach a sporting team. There are never enough parents to get behind local sporting teams. Introduce what you have learned about leadership and team spirit to a group of kids wanting to play sport.

Run a free seminar about something you know about—maybe running your own business. If you have managed to survive for a while you are suitably qualified to share your views with others.

Whatever interest grabs you, being prepared to share your knowledge and experience is a good way to become a better corporate citizen.

What can you do today?

Make up a list of ways you can share your knowledge and experience with other people in your local community. Then get on the telephone and turn the list into reality.

#75 Encourage your staff to be good corporate citizens

If you are prepared to be a good corporate citizen your staff will be more likely to want to get involved as well. Make it easy for them to do this and encourage them to participate. It is important not to be threatening or intimidating—some people just don't want to get involved and that is fine. They should not feel like their job is not secure if they don't.

What you are trying to do is to provide the right environment for your staff to feel they would like to get involved. This may mean making a few allowances for them giving up their time, it may even mean some financial support; for example, if a group of your staff want to enter a fun run, offer to sponsor them.

Community involvement is a great team building exercise and it is rewarding in a lot of ways—not the least of which is the realisation that as an individual you can really make a difference. Provide the right working environment and most workplaces will automatically produce some community minded individuals who will drive the process from within. Encourage and support them as much as you feel able and recognise their efforts.

What can you do today?

Are there ways you could be more encouraging of your staff to help them become better corporate citizens? Why not get your team in and ask them? If you already have a proactive team who are heavily involved in the community, can you acknowledge their efforts more?

#76 Some things can't be measured in dollars and cents

In every marketing plan I write I always make a point of encouraging the business to become more involved in their community. I outline the importance of being a good corporate citizen and the fact that consumers these days want to deal with businesses actively involved in their community.

Some business owners just don't get it. They ask questions like, 'How much free publicity will I get?' or, 'How many new customers will it get me?' or, 'How much will this add to my bottom line?' Some things simply can't be measured in dollars and cents and community involvement is certainly one of those things.

I can't tell you how much more money it will make you, but I can tell you there are a lot of consumers out there making conscious decisions about where they will spend their money. Given the choice between spending it on a business that plays an active role in the community and one that doesn't, what choice do you think they will make?

Apart from that concept alone—what about doing the right thing and having integrity. You need to think much deeper than just returns on investment. Even the largest organisations in the world have realised this and they are going to great lengths to show the world both corporate compassion and corporate responsibility.

This is why I have no problem with businesses that promote themselves as being actively involved in their community; in fact I recommend they do. If it means the community wins, that is all that matters. We are all charged with the responsibility of making the world a better place.

What can you do today?

If you find yourself asking questions about returns on investment when it comes to helping to build a better community you need to develop a measuring system other than money. Call it karma or whatever you like and accept this is as equally relevant a currency as money, and in many ways it is much better.

#77 Invest in the future of your industry

Investing your time, energy and even possibly some money into the future of your industry is another part of being a good corporate citizen. Clearly it is different to helping a charity or another community based organisation but it is just as important.

One example I can talk about is a relationship I have with my local university. They have a good business faculty with a strong bent towards marketing. I regularly give guest lectures, appraise projects or assignments and invite students to work in my office to get experience. I gladly give my time freely as I believe very strongly in putting back into my industry and also providing assistance to the next generation coming through.

Too many people have a 'What's in it for me?' approach to business. Truly successful people are always prepared to give of themselves as they understand the big picture.

What can you do today?

Look for ways you can support the future of your own industry. Ask other people in your industry what they do and how you can help or get involved.

#78 Offer praise wherever possible to other members of the community

I recently helped plan a large outdoor concert where all of the funds raised went to an organisation called Lifeline. Lifeline does an amazing job in the community, mainly focusing on its 24-hour telephone crisis line for people who need someone to talk to in a dark period of their lives. The concert was great and the event was considered a success on many different levels.

A few days later I received a letter in the mail from an old lady thanking me for getting involved in this concert. She explained how Lifeline had helped her when she had lost her husband to cancer. She was feeling very alone and had seriously contemplated committing suicide. I couldn't help but have tears rolling down my face as I realised the human side of getting behind my community.

Since that day I have made an effort to drop a short letter or email to people who I see playing an active role in making my community a better place to be. Sometimes it's just to say thank you, sometimes it is more personal where I tell them of an experience I had, just like the lady who wrote to me.

Taking the time to say thank you to people who give tirelessly of themselves is a good thing to do. It will mean a lot to them. They certainly don't expect it but I am sure they appreciate it—I certainly do.

What can you do today?

The very next time you read about someone who has gone out of their way to help make your community a better place, do some detective work and track down their address and send them a card or a thank you letter.

#79 Don't be afraid to tell people you are a good corporate citizen

Just as I feel it is important to be a good corporate citizen I certainly don't see anything wrong with telling your customers about it. In fact, I strongly recommend that you do.

Put the certificates on the wall in a public place. Include what you do in your company profile or on your website. Larger organisations actually make up entire brochures showing what they do in their community; this is an excellent idea, especially as consumers are looking to do business with companies that care about the communities that they operate in.

As explained earlier in this section, consumers want to deal with companies that are good corporate citizens and it is up to the business to let them know. Don't be afraid to blow your own trumpet and say you are actively involved in your community—it is something to be proud of, not embarrassed about.

Don't think it is just about big things either. Something as small as donating a few dollars to a local charity is significant in the scheme of things and it is relevant. Giving too much may cause your business to get into financial difficulties, which does no good to anyone. Get involved at a level you can manage easily, both financially and time wise.

Do what you can and be prepared to let your customers know what you do. They will appreciate it and you for making their community a better place to live, regardless of the size of your contribution.

What can you do today?

How do you let your customers know that you play an active role in the community? Today is the day to put the certificate on the wall or include your community involvement on your website or in your promotional material.

#80 Make up a plan to make you the ultimate corporate citizen

Like any component of a successful business, the better you plan the greater your chances of succeeding. The same principle applies to the goal of becoming the ultimate corporate citizen. Making up a plan for how you and your business will play an active role in your community is a wise choice of action.

This plan should address:

* which types of organisations you would like to get involved with
* how much time each week you can spare
* how much financial support you can afford to give
* what products and services you offer (remembering, they still have cost)
* ways to encourage your staff to get involved
* specific details about how you will tell your customers you are community spirited
* how you will recognise other people in the community who get involved
* how you can share your own knowledge and experience.

This doesn't need to be a big and in-depth plan, just a few pages addressing each of the questions above. Start a file called 'Becoming the Ultimate Corporate Citizen' and you are well and truly on your way to achieving this goal.

Once you have your plan in place, take the time to share it with your staff. They will, after all, be playing an important role.

What can you do today?

Develop your own plan to become the 'Ultimate Corporate Citizen'.

Action pages

Things I need to do to make my business more successful.
71 Be involved in the community where you do business
Action required right now

....
....
....
....

Completed (date, time and by whom)

....
....

72 Look for opportunities outside of the normal
Action required right now

....
....
....
....

Completed (date, time and by whom)

....
....

73 Stand up and be counted
Action required right now

....
....
....
....
....

Completed (date, time and by whom)

. . . .

. . . .

74 Share your knowledge and experience with others
Action required right now

. . . .

. . . .

. . . .

. . . .

Completed (date, time and by whom)

. . . .

. . . .

75 Encourage your staff to be good corporate citizens
Action required right now

. . . .

. . . .

. . . .

. . . .

Completed (date, time and by whom)

. . . .

. . . .

76 Some things can't be measured in dollars and cents
Action required right now

. . . .

. . . .

. . . .

. . . .

. . . .

Completed (date, time and by whom)

. . . .

. . . .

 # 77 Invest in the future of your industry
Action required right now

. . . .

. . . .

. . . .

. . . .

Completed (date, time and by whom)

. . . .

. . . .

 # 78 Offer praise wherever possible to other members of the community
Action required right now

. . . .

. . . .

. . . .

. . . .

Completed (date, time and by whom)

. . . .

. . . .

 # 79 Don't be afraid to tell people you are a good corporate citizen
Action required right now

. . . .

. . . .

. . . .

Completed (date, time and by whom)

. . . .

. . . .

80 Make up a plan to make you the ultimate corporate citizen

Action required right now

. . . .

. . . .

. . . .

. . . .

Completed (date, time and by whom)

. . . .

. . . .

Brainstorming pages

Use these pages to write notes, comments, ideas or things to do regarding the preceding section. The aim is to improve your business a little every day, to make it more successful and for you to enjoy being an entrepreneur.

....

....

....

....

....

....

....

....

....

....

....

....

....

....

....

....

....

....

....

....

....

....

'In every society there are human "benchmarks"—
certain individuals whose behaviour
becomes the model for everyone else—
shining examples that others admire and emulate.
We call these individuals "class acts".'

Dan Sullivan, co-founder and President, The Strategic Coach

10 | Making yourself as impressive as your business

When running a business of any size or in any industry it is easy to focus all your attention on the business and not a lot on yourself. The people I have encountered who have built amazing businesses all invest as much in themselves as they do in their businesses. This doesn't just mean financially; it means energy, it means personal development, it means helping others to grow. Putting all of your resources into your business is an easy trap, one I have certainly fallen into in the past. When you start to balance your life the results are often quite astonishing. Your business thrives and so does your life. You enjoy what you do a lot more. Your decisions are better and you portray a feeling of success that attracts success into your life. This section will look at ways to help you to become as impressive as your business.

81   Appearances are everything
82   Have a strong moral code—with no shades of grey
83   Be a fair negotiator
84   Be more than your business
85   Have a life outside of your business
86   Be a supporter of other business associates
87   Mix with people you can learn from

88   Make decisions—procrastination is a killer
89   Commit to improving your business skills daily
90   Don't be a victim (and keep people who play victim out of your life)

#81 Appearances are everything

Appearances are everything is an old saying which, from my own experience, I don't think is necessarily 100 per cent correct but I have no doubt that appearances are very important. In my dealings with successful entrepreneurs they generally look the part. They have an air of confidence about them and they feel successful.

I had this drummed into me at an early age. If you want to succeed at what you do you need to look the part: dress appropriately, be groomed appropriately, drive an appropriate car and so on. If you are trying to portray yourself as a successful business owner, make yourself look successful.

Think back to the last time you walked into a business that looked like it was on skid row. Not very inspiring, was it? You certainly don't get a feeling of confidence from a business like this. The same can apply to an individual. If you want your customers to have confidence in you then look the part. This applies not only to you but to anyone representing your business.

Uniforms should always be neat and tidy, well ironed and of course clean. Company vehicles should be well maintained and clean. Crumpled, worn-out uniforms and beaten up company cars send a clear message: business is either struggling or the owners just don't care—both normally go hand in hand.

I recently pulled up at a set of traffic lights and waiting next to me was one of the most beat up and filthy cars I had seen in a long time. Clouds of smoke were billowing out from the engine and the driver was choking back a cigarette. All over this car were signs promoting a business, which I gather owned the car. They were selling the virtues of filtered water as a means of living a healthier life. There is no way I would ever buy filtered water from this company. If their vehicle is like this what must their end product be like?

We all make these assumptions based on appearances. To succeed at what you do look the part and your customers will know that you take your business seriously.

What can you do today?

Make a list of five ways you can improve either your appearance or the appearance of some aspects of your business and action them. It might mean buying some new clothes, or getting uniforms or having the company car detailed.

#82 Have a strong moral code—with no shades of grey

How many examples do you know of high-profile people who were shining stars but became corporate disgraces? It really is quite disheartening when business leaders once featured on the front of dozens of major magazines are just a few years later being dragged into court and often prison. Why does this happen? How can they have fallen? What corrupted them?

In reality the answer is most likely that they were always corruptible. It's often the case that there were never enough people looking closely enough to catch them out earlier. A friend of mine was once listed as one of the Top 500 wealthiest people in Australia. He told me that from that day on every government organisation went through every business dealing he ever had with a fine-tooth comb. He had nothing to worry about, he is a very honest man, but it was disconcerting to say the least.

We all need to live by a strong moral code. Be very clear about what is right and what is wrong. There should be no shades of grey because often these are places where you falter. What is your moral code? Do you have situations that you have to deal with which could be considered grey?

Of course there are differences between moral, ethical and legal codes, but in reality they are closely linked. Once you cross a line, it is a lot easier to keep crossing it and most offenders do.

My philosophy is simple—I will not do anything, ever, that can come back and haunt me. I don't want to ever leave my office with a towel over my head scurrying away from a host of reporters. Apart from the devastating impact it has on your fashion sense it ruins lives, often those of the innocent parties.

What can you do today?

What is your moral code? Do you have areas of grey that need to be clarified once and for all? If you do, clarify them today—even if the ramifications are scary.

#83 Be a fair negotiator

There is a saying that for a negotiation to work, all parties need to win. The level of the win varies, but that is the ideal outcome. Some people adopt an egotistical stance of having to win everything at any cost whenever they enter a negotiation. We all know these kinds of people. They negotiate on the purchase of a bus ticket. They are obsessed with the win, to the point where they spend their life burning other people and, eventually, people don't want to deal with them.

Negotiating is a part of life. In business we need to be good negotiators to make sure we can run our businesses as profitably as possible. But the key word here is fair. I have to negotiate with suppliers, such as graphic designers, media outlets, printers and subcontractors. I want to have a good relationship with these companies and I want them to do the best job possible for my clients. If I negotiate them down on price to the point where the project is only marginally profitable, they will lose interest, I will get a marginal quality job from them and the loser is my client.

I make it clear to my clients from the start: we want to do the best job at the fairest price. If they want a cheaper job done, they have to go somewhere else. This philosophy has enabled me to build an excellent network of suppliers who do a great job every time. They make good money out of each project, my company makes good money and the client gets the best end result possible.

What can you do today?

What is your philosophy towards negotiating? Are you a fair negotiator or a win-at-any-cost one? The next time you find yourself preparing to enter a negotiation, at any level, take a few minutes to decide how you think all parties can win and work towards this end result. It will make the whole interaction much more enjoyable and the end result will be much better for all parties involved.

#84 Be more than your business

Businesses come and go—what you are doing today is unlikely to be what you will be doing in ten years' time. You are the most significant asset in your life and it is important to realise this.

I encounter a lot of people who become their business—it is everything, from their waking moment in the morning to their last thought at night (and often it fills their dreams). When they no longer have this business their life falls apart. They don't know what to do, their life feels empty and dissatisfaction and depression can set in.

Look at the lives of a few high-profile entrepreneurs. Rarely do they have only one business interest. They may start new businesses, sell old ones, go broke in some, do a joint venture in others—they are not attached to one business. They are passionate about what they do but they realise they are the resource and the skill centre used to make the other businesses work. They are more than any of the businesses that they own.

Whatever you are doing, there is life after your current business. For this reason you need to be more than your business. You need to have more substance, more interests, more beliefs and more of a long-term view about how you fit into your business life. Don't let your business consume or control you—you are in the driving seat, not the other way around.

What can you do today?

Ponder this thought—what would you do if you got a letter in the mail that said you had to close down your business in 24 hours? How would you cope? What would you do next? An interesting situation to spend a few minutes considering.

#85 Have a life outside of your business

We all get absorbed in our businesses and as I have discussed elsewhere in this book, there is a need for this level of passion and commitment. For many entrepreneurs it comes naturally, but balancing your work life with your personal life can be difficult.

A few years ago I found myself running a growing business. While it wasn't the success I wanted it to be it was well and truly on the way. I had the philosophy that the harder I worked the closer I would be to realising the true potential of the business. So work I did.

Every day I arrived around 6 a.m. and left around 7 or 8 at night. I worked seven days a week and I rarely took a day off. I think I became obsessed with what I was doing and this level of obsession is unhealthy. I gained a lot of weight, had a lot of stress, never exercised and I was always tired and run down. A changing point for me came when my sister died suddenly from a heart attack at the age of 35. I realised I was heading down the same path and I was 33. So I decided to change.

It didn't happen overnight and I have to work on it to this day. But now I feel my life is far more balanced than it has been in a long time. I have lost about 30 kilograms, I work out with a personal trainer a couple of times every week, I do yoga as often as possible and I feel great. I start work at about 8 a.m. after having a good breakfast, something I never used to do. I always stop and have a good lunch. I leave the office by about 5.30 p.m. most days. I rarely work on weekends unless it is absolutely necessary and, then, only if it is work I enjoy doing, like writing books. I pack a lot more into my working day. I am busier now than I have ever been but I have very clear boundaries on when work starts and finishes and where my personal life starts and finishes.

At first the hardest part was to remember what I liked to do; recreation was a strange feeling and one I struggled with.

So I made a list of the things I really enjoyed doing—everything from going out to dinner, to seeing a movie, camping, fishing, reading and most normal types of recreational pursuit. I put this list in the front of my diary and whenever I felt lost about how to spend my time off I pulled out my list, picked out one of the things I really enjoyed doing and I did it.

Over time, my life has got back in balance and I feel sensational. Sure I have periods when it is chaotic, stressful and challenging, but they are much fewer and faurther between than before. I run my business better, and there is a good chance I will live longer. I have a lot more friends outside of my business world and they keep my feet firmly planted on the ground.

We all need to have a life outside of our businesses as this is what life is all about. If you have forgotten how, make up your own list, work out how to spend less time at work, don't hide behind the excuse that you have to be there. Really, if you have to work seven days a week in your business is it really that profitable? Is it viable? Maybe you should be doing something else altogether (this may open a can of worms but I recommend that you read *101 Ways to Have a Business and a Life* to investigate this issue a little more).

What can you do today?

If your life isn't balanced the way you would like it to be, take steps to change things today. Make a list of the things you used to enjoy doing (and to be even a little more in your face write next to each one the last time you did it). Ring the local gym and get a personal trainer. Do a course that interests you which has nothing to do with business. Remember, radical changes like this tend to require a lot of work to make them stick. If you set unreasonable goals it is unlikely to happen, so take small steps and work towards your ideal lifestyle.

#86 Be a supporter of other business associates

We all want other people to promote our businesses and to refer customers to us but do we reciprocate and recommend our supporters' businesses to our clients? Doing this often takes a conscious effort but after a while it becomes second nature.

Any kind of recommendation or referral should be a two-way street if possible. Be clear about which businesses you would like to support and promote them accordingly. It might be quite formal, where you agree to distribute each other's promotional material or do joint advertising or marketing campaigns, or it might be a little more informal—when the opportunity arises you may promote your associates' businesses by word of mouth to your customers.

I have found that the more support I give to other people's businesses the more I get back in return. I don't do it for this reason, that's just an added bonus. I genuinely want to see these people succeed in what they do and if I can play a small role by referring business to them I will do so gladly.

I also encourage my staff to refer businesses wherever possible.

Just like asking your customers to tell their family and friends about what you do, imagine how many referrals will start coming your way if your business associates are doing the same thing. This really is the way of the future for building businesses as it is harder for advertising to make an impact and it is also getting more costly. Direct recommendations are perfect and they are free—the ideal marketing tool.

Think about the people who refer your business. Can you possibly be more active in promoting their businesses? Do it for the right reasons and enjoy the benefits. If you are not 100 per cent sure what they actually do, ask them to come and tell you and your staff so you are completely informed.

What can you do today?

Make a list of businesses you would like to promote. Keep their contact details close to the telephone and wherever possible refer them to your customers as your 'partner' businesses. Try to do this once per day, every day of the coming week. After a little while it will become a habit.

#87 Mix with people you can learn from

Most entrepreneurs are fairly up-beat kind of people. They are keen to learn and equally keen to pass on their knowledge. Mixing with people who you can learn from is a great way to develop your own business skills and also to pass on your own experiences to help others.

If you mix with smart, successful, enthusiastic people you will become like them if you aren't already. If you are struggling and feeling a little flat, spending time around these people will pick you up and you will do the same for them.

For me I love nothing better than mixing with a group of people who I find stimulating and interesting. Likewise I find nothing worse than mixing with a group of negative, depressed, lacklustre individuals who blame the world for their woes.

Where do you find this group of inspirational souls to mix with? Talk to people you admire and see what they do. I have found that people like this are already meeting each other either formally or informally all the time. They don't make a big deal about it, they just do it—a reflection of their lives in general. Or make your own group if you can't find one.

With the advent of Internet chat rooms and teleconferencing you don't even need to be in the same country any more, although it's easier and much nicer to be able to meet face to face. I know a number of people who have formed their own group, consisting of about six people of varying business backgrounds. They meet twelve times every year and spend two sessions brainstorming each of the businesses owned by the people attending. So sometimes you are giving advice, sometimes you are receiving advice, but there is a lot of overlap as often the good advice for another business is just as applicable for your business.

What can you do today?

What type of people do you spend your time with? Are they positive and good for you or are they a negative influence? Why not set up your own mentoring group today? Call five associates that you respect and ask them to be involved.

#88 Make decisions—procrastination is a killer

Personally I find the busier I become, the harder it is to make a decision. I get bombarded with literally hundreds of messages every day, from the fax, the phone, email, letters and internally from my team. There is so much to do that finding the time to make a decision on any one thing can be really difficult. But if I don't make decisions, my workload backs up, my clients get frustrated and so do my staff.

A friend of mine who has run some very large corporations pulled me aside a little while ago and gave me some important advice. She said I had to learn to start making decisions right now; not to keep putting them on the backburner for when I would have more time to think about them. If I did all I would do is end up with an ever expanding list of 'decisions to be made', which I would never get to the end of. I took her advice and she was spot on.

I now make decisions on the spot as often as possible. Some things need a little more time to ponder but in reality the vast majority of my decisions are simple yes or no decisions that someone else needs to action. This has had quite an amazing flow on to my daily workload: it seems I have a lot less to do, I don't go home with a never ending list of things to think about and everyone I deal with is happier because they are getting their decisions quickly.

Sure sometimes I make the wrong decisions, but that happened before as well. We all get it right sometimes and wrong at others but I think the number of wrong decisions I make has declined significantly.

What can you do today?

Do you procrastinate when it comes to making decisions? End that today.

#89 Commit to improving your business skills daily

Passionate entrepreneurs seem to have this never ending thirst for ways to do what they do better. They are not afraid to ask questions, to read books, to go to seminars or to learn how to do what they do better. This commitment shines through because they end up putting what they learn into practice.

My guess is that you fit into this category as well, otherwise you wouldn't have invested in this book. But how can you assimilate everything that is on offer considering the mass of information available today and still find the time to run your business and have a life outside of work? Personally I break it into small bite-sized chunks. My aim is to learn how to do two things better—one for business and one for my personal life—every day of the week.

If I am reading a book on self improvement or business my aim is to find one point I can use today and incorporate that into my business life every day from now on. The same applies to my own personal development—all I want is one point, but I want one every single day of my life.

It is like going to a seminar on business development. It is easy to be bombarded with fifty great things you can do but let's be honest, how many will you get around to actioning? Probably none because the task is too daunting. But if you go into the seminar with a very clear expectation—to take one suggestion that has struck a chord with you and apply it to your business life right now—your chances of achieving this are much higher. I have literally hundreds of business and self-development books. I have read them all and for the most part they are amazing. Filled with thousands of superb ideas and recommendations, but what use are they if none of them are converted into action by me?

Commit to improving your business and life skills in small manageable chunks. It works for me, and hopefully it will work for you.

What can you do today?

Decide what achievable action you will take to improve your business skills (and hopefully your life skills) on a daily basis. Remember, 'achievable' is the key word here.

#90 Don't be a victim (and keep people who play victim out of your life)

I had one of those unusual childhoods: I grew up as an orphan, living with a host of different people during my formative years—some people were great, some not so great. I had a lot of violence inflicted upon me. I was in situations where I trusted people that I shouldn't have. I knew a lot of people with whom I developed close bonds but they died. But not once have I ever felt like a victim.

Life throws different blows at all of us and we can choose to focus on these or we can focus on the good things that happen. I choose to focus on the good. I am not saying for a second there haven't been times when the going got rough, but focusing on the good got me through a lot of situations and a challenging start to life that many others may not have survived. As a result, I am compassionate and empathetic with anyone going through a rocky patch.

Some people, though, wallow in the role of the victim— everything bad is someone else's fault and they are going to wear the title of 'victim' with pride. Victims attract other victims and the cycle becomes self-perpetuating. Ironically, I have found that the people who may have the most right to wear a 'victim' badge rarely do. They are too busy getting on with life.

The easiest thing for me to do would be to store anger and resentment against a host of people who either hurt me, abandoned me or used me. But without those people I wouldn't have turned out who I am today—and I am pretty darn happy with who I am today.

We all face trying times, family problems, relationship problems, money problems and health problems—that is life. But playing victim won't make them go away. Focus on the good things in your life, learn from your experiences and move on. Keep people who play victim out of your life and you will

soon find positive and enthusiastic people will replace them—
and your life will become a lot better.

What can you do today?

Are you playing victim in your life? Are there people around
you who support the victim mentality? Well, today is the
day to throw the victim badge away and get on with your
life.

Action pages

Things I need to do to make my business more successful.
81 Appearances are everything
Action required right now

....

....

....

....

Completed (date, time and by whom)

....

....

82 Have a strong moral code—with no shades of grey
Action required right now

....

....

....

....

Completed (date, time and by whom)

....

....

83 Be a fair negotiator
Action required right now

....

....

....

....

....

Completed (date, time and by whom)

....

....

84 Be more than your business
Action required right now

....

....

....

....

Completed (date, time and by whom)

....

....

85 Have a life outside of your business
Action required right now

....

....

....

....

Completed (date, time and by whom)

....

....

86 Be a supporter of other business associates
Action required right now

....

....

....

....

....

Completed (date, time and by whom)

. . . .

. . . .

87 Mix with people you can learn from
Action required right now

. . . .

. . . .

. . . .

. . . .

Completed (date, time and by whom)

. . . .

. . . .

88 Make decisions—procrastination is a killer
Action required right now

. . . .

. . . .

. . . .

. . . .

Completed (date, time and by whom)

. . . .

. . . .

89 Commit to improving your business skills daily
Action required right now

. . . .

. . . .

. . . .

. . . .

. . . .

Completed (date, time and by whom)

....

....

90 Don't be a victim (and keep people who play victim out of your life)
Action required right now

....

....

....

....

Completed (date, time and by whom)

....

....

Brainstorming page

Use this page to write notes, comments, ideas or things to do regarding the preceding section. The aim is to improve your business a little every day, to make it more successful and for you to enjoy being an entrepreneur.

....
....
....
....
....
....
....
....
....
....
....
....
....
....
....
....
....
....
....
....
....
....

'A pessimist sees the difficulty in every opportunity; an optimist sees the opportunity in every difficulty.'

Winston Churchill

11 | Set the pace for your competitors to follow

At the start of *101 Secrets to Building a Winning Business* I explained my thoughts on the future of business. The most obvious and significant piece of advice I can offer is that modern business is extremely competitive and this is a factor that is only going to increase. We all have to deal with competition and I believe this is a good thing, not a bad thing. Competition keeps us trying to be better, it stops us from becoming complacent and it fuels the drive to make our business better than the rest. I believe customers like the concept of competition. Apart from the obvious reason that it tends to make things more affordable, it also gives people a choice and we all like to have a choice.

There are two ways to look at a highly competitive market: it can be stressful and difficult to make a business successful or it can be an amazing opportunity to drive your business forward. There have been countless examples of businesses entering highly competitive markets and succeeding at quite amazing levels. In Australia the greatest example of this in recent times was the introduction of Virgin Blue, the successful ticket discounting airline. Virgin Blue quite literally changed the aviation industry in Australia by shaking up an industry locked into the 'old way' of doing things and in the process managed to build a strong and loyal clientele in a short amount of time by being innovative. As a by-product, it also made money—something most airlines in the world seem to struggle to do. The same thing has happened for them in the US and UK markets.

The following tips and recommendations are designed to show you how to use your competition to make your business a winning one.

\# 91 Believe you are the best and you will become the best

\# 92 Enter your business in awards whenever possible

\# 93 Get your name in print—there are plenty of opportunities

\# 94 Be prepared to get up in front of a crowd—challenge yourself

\# 95 Being a green business is good for business

\# 96 Be supportive of competitors—even if it is one-sided

\# 97 Spend time researching your industry online

\# 98 Allow plenty of time to think—and less time to do

\# 99 Learn from your mistakes

\# 100 Even better, learn from your competitors' mistakes

\# 101 Don't become obsessed with your competitors

#91 Believe you are the best and you will become the best

Being the best at what you do has to start with a very firm and genuine belief you can be the best. If you start your business with the aim of being as good as your competitors that is very noble but far too limiting.

A long time ago I had a business that was really struggling. A friend sat me down and explained in very simple terms that to be the best you have to do everything better than the competition. It's a fairly logical thought but it is one that is often not thought through. Being the best may mean shaking old traditions and beliefs and stepping outside of your comfort zone, perhaps redefining what is considered the norm in your chosen industry. Believing you are the best is the starting point: from here you need to implement the right actions to make sure you actually are the best at what you do and that you can deliver on your promise.

With my business at the time, this change in thinking was really the starting point I needed to untangle the mess I had created, and to put a very clear goal and objective into place. This desire to be the best needs to be imparted to your staff, your suppliers and your customers. Sure, there will be hurdles to cross, mistakes made and lessons learnt, but you will be heading in the right direction.

What can you do today?

Get a big sheet of paper and write your commitment statement on it: 'I am going to make this the BEST .... [whatever your business is]' and sign your name to this commitment. Put your statement on the wall in your office or place it in a prominent position— where you'll see it constantly.

#92 Enter your business in awards whenever possible

Winning an award is great for business. It gives you recognition, it gives your customers faith in what you do and it motivates the entire team. Everyone loves a winner. There are lots of different awards being run all the time. Some are industry specific, some are geographically specific—it doesn't really matter, an award is an award.

Many businesses don't bother entering awards because it can take up quite a bit of time actually filling in the submissions. There are often lots of questions that need to be answered and these can require a reasonable amount of attention. But entering awards should be considered a marketing activity.

If you are looking for a competitive advantage, being an award winner is certainly one very good boost. If you are fortunate enough to win an award make sure you let everyone know. Put the certificate on your office wall in a prominent place, and make mention of the award on your website and on all of your promotional material. Keeping the certificate in the bottom drawer really is a waste of time and a missed golden opportunity.

I always recommend my clients enter awards wherever possible and those that win really do get quite a lift.

What can you do today?

Is there a submission for an award that you can start working on today? If you are not sure, contact your local government-based Business Advisory Service—they normally know all about these types of things and they can often even help you to prepare your submission.

#93 Get your name in print — there are plenty of opportunities

There are many benefits from having your name in print (and by print these days I mean in print publications or online). It gives you and your business a lot of credibility, it reinforces to your customers that you know what you are talking about and it generates new business from people who like what you say. The more your name appears in print the more it will continue to appear as your reputation grows.

There are more opportunities to get your name in print today than ever before. There are so many newspapers and magazines and they all need content. If the editors and journalists can find industry leaders who are prepared to comment on relevant stories or to submit articles there is a good chance those leaders will be published in some format.

The best way to get your name into print is to supply a brief profile outlining who you are and what you do, specifically what areas you feel you're able to offer an informed comment on to the various publications. It is also a good idea to supply a high resolution electronic version of your photograph (taken professionally) so the publication can publish it with any associated stories.

There are also lots of freelance journalists who are looking for subjects to write articles about. Check the local newspapers and magazines for the names of specific journalists and send them your profile and associated information.

This kind of exposure is relevant at any level—either nationally, internationally or even on the smaller local level. All it takes is a little bit of courage to actually submit your information and accept the fact that you are good at what you do. You are just as qualified as anyone in your industry to make comments.

What can you do today?

Today is a good day to arrange your profile kit and send it out to a number of publications. Start small if that makes you feel more comfortable and build up to the larger, wider-scale opportunities as your confidence grows.

#94 Be prepared to get up in front of a crowd— challenge yourself

For many people the thought of a slow and painful death is preferable to having to stand in front of a crowd and give a talk. As an experienced public speaker I can really relate to this. There are still times when I break into a cold sweat before going on stage. Sometimes it is harder to stand and present in front of a group of 20 people than it is to talk in front of 1000 people. For most of us it is challenging.

I did my first public speaking course when I was at high school and I must say I am very glad I did. I also like to do refreshers every once in a while as I am firmly committed to improving my skills as a public speaker. The opportunities that public speaking presents are considerable and it gives you the opportunity to share your expertise in your chosen field.

There are many situations that call on people to present in a group situation and if you let people know you are prepared to do it, more opportunities will come your way. So take the challenge, face the fear and go for it.

What can you do today?

Anyone can become a better public speaker. Like most skills, though, we need to be taught how. Sign up for a public speaking course that will teach you how to overcome nerves and other insecurities and that will enable you to get up in front of a group of people and share your own knowledge and experiences. Lots of businesses offer these courses. Toast Masters International is one of the most renowned organisations for these types of things but there are plenty to choose from in every country. Even if you are an experienced public speaker your skills can only get better by doing a course like this.

#95 Being a green business is good for business

Running a successful business certainly covers a lot of ground. So far we have discussed corporate imaging, building relationships, customer service, marketing and a host of other topics. But being committed to running an environmentally responsible business is not only good for the environment, it is good for the bank balance—that is a relationship often overlooked.

I have had quite a lot of experience marketing environmentally focused businesses and this is a topic I am passionate about. The point which often amazes me is that green consumers (those who make many of their buying decisions based on environmental responsibility) are growing in numbers rapidly; they are prepared to pay more for green products and services and they are informed and intelligent about those products. Best of all, they are easy to market to because they are actively looking for environmentally responsible products and services.

If your business is more environmentally aware and responsible than your competitors you will attract customers on this point of difference alone. Of course, if you are an environmentally responsible business you need to tell your customers how you are and what your commitment is.

One excellent example of this is the Body Shop. This impressive organisation has grown to be a leader in beauty products with the main sales point being that the business will not sell any products that don't fit into its stringent corporate philosophy on environmental responsibility and respect for animals. Consumers know that if they purchase a Body Shop product they can rest assured that it has not been tested on animals, a rainforest has not been cut down to produce it or a five-year-old child used in the manufacturing process.

There are lots of ways to be green, far too many to list here. Look at your business from every possible angle and start with small changes, building up to much larger and more significant changes. When your business is environmentally aware you will reap both the moral and financial rewards. One important note here though is, if you are running an environmentally responsible business take the time to explain to your customers what you do to adhere to this code. This can be in your promotional material, on your website or on a sign in your business. Make sure your staff know your philosophy and your commitment.

What can you do today?

Sit down and make a list of five things you could do today to make your business more environmentally responsible. Then make them happen. Develop your own environmental philosophy and tell your customers what it is.

#96 Be supportive of competitors—even if it is one-sided

Taking a mature approach to your competitors is a very positive business attribute, even if it isn't reciprocated. In my home town there are quite a few marketing companies, all competing for the same clients, but we have developed a very positive network of referrals and support. My business isn't suited for all clients and if I recognise that a competitor will be better matched to a potential client's needs I have no hesitation in recommending them for the job. In fact, I have offered marketing advice on a professional basis to a number of my competitors; likewise I have used their services when I needed them for my own business.

True success comes from rising above petty points of difference and working towards providing the best products and services from the industry as a whole. The more you work with your competitors the more you will benefit.

I have experienced this first hand in the tourism industry. I live in Cairns, a regional city in Australia, which is the main stepping off point for the Great Barrier Reef. Every year we have about two million tourists coming to our city to enjoy the natural attractions. As you can imagine, the tourism industry is well established, mature and sophisticated. There are hundreds of different tours, hotels, attractions and specialised tourism related retailers. There is also a strong underlying current where most of these businesses will work together to promote tourism in the region, even if their particular business doesn't directly benefit from the promotion. The aim is to attract more tourists—full stop.

It can be very reassuring to sit down with your competitors and talk about business in general. It is nice to know the trials and tribulations you face are also faced by your competitors. But it takes one person to extend the olive branch or to open communication channels. If you already have good relationships with your competitors what can you do to make them even better?

What can you do today?

Make a list of your competitors and write down one sentence that best describes your relationship with each of these businesses. Then write another sentence to say what you could do to have a better relationship.

#97 Spend time researching your industry online

Interestingly this is often an idea overlooked by business owners. It is a very good exercise to spend some time seeing how your industry operates in other countries. Checking out websites from around the world can give you a wealth of information with only a small amount of time spent researching.

The more you explore the more you will find. Use search engines to get the process started but also track down the web addresses of similar companies you may have come across in trade publications.

Not only will you pick up good ideas on building your business but you will more than likely find valuable information about industry trends that could have an impact on your business. If you find out about these trends before your competitors do, your business will be well out in front of the field.

To take this point a little further, it is helpful to print out information you find on the net. Often when you are in a surfing frenzy it is easy to get sidetracked. Before you know you forget about something you came across earlier. Collect the information and start a file. Much of the information you come across could probably be distributed among your staff— encourage them to learn from your research.

Spending time to see how other people do the same thing as you is time well spent. Smart entrepreneurs know the value of research and they never begrudge spending time on it. Winning businesses are always one step ahead of their competitors.

What can you do today?

Spend 30 minutes today researching your industry online. Set yourself a challenge to find out something you didn't know before. Start a file and allocate a certain time each week to do nothing but surf the web for research.

#98 Allow plenty of time to think — and less time to do

Another one of the themes I talk about a lot is the issue of time and the way we all seem to be locked into a constant battle to manage our time effectively. In my mind the most serious side effect of this time battle is that we simply don't find the time to stop and think about our business. We are too busy doing and not busy enough thinking. Taking time out to do nothing but think about your business is therapeutic and beneficial but only if we can make it good quality time.

We all think differently, some people think best in the morning; some at night. Some people need to be in the office to get into the right frame of mind, others need to get away from the office. Personally I think best on a long drive. Every few weeks I jump into my car, grab my mini cassette recorder and go for a long drive, maybe for two or three hours up into the mountains near where I live. There are beautiful, rolling green hills, lush rainforest, lakes and normally not a lot of traffic. With the exception of the odd kangaroo bounding across the road, it is relaxing and I find that as soon as I leave the outskirts of town my mind relaxes and I can start to think more clearly. As I drive along I think about the issues at the forefront of my mind, those that are most pressing. As the kilometres roll by these issues tend to resolve themselves and I either record notes or jot down my thoughts and ideas in my notebook. By the end of my outing I not only feel relaxed, I also feel much clearer and more focused. I have a solution to the issues which I can take back to work and apply on the spot.

This works for me; it might not for you, but what is important here is to find what works for you and use it as often as you can. Sure there is never enough time but you have to make time to think about your business to move it forward, otherwise you may end up stuck in a never changing cycle where business problems are never resolved and opportunities missed because you are too busy just doing the day to day stuff.

What can you do today?

Try to identify when you do your best thinking. Make a list of issues you are struggling to resolve and lock in some time to just think about them. After a while this will become habit forming and you will look forward to these thinking sessions because you will achieve positive results and your business will move forward.

#99 Learn from your mistakes

Business experience is mostly about learning through the mistakes we make. I know I have made far more than my fair share, but as the years go by I am getting a little smarter and learning the lessons a lot quicker.

There wouldn't be many successful entrepreneurs who could say they have a mistake-free background. In fact, I would be impressed to meet one and that is what makes entrepreneurs so amazing. When they get it wrong, they pick themselves up, dust themselves off and get on with the next opportunity at hand.

We all make mistakes and we all will continue to make mistakes—the trick is to learn your lesson and move on. If you make a business mistake and it costs you money, there is no doubt it will stay in your mind for a long time to come and that is not a bad thing. There is no point crucifying yourself; after all, even the most experienced and high-profile entrepreneurs end up explaining where they went wrong at some stage. Punishing yourself more than necessary is not only non-productive it can also shake your confidence and increase your chances of making more mistakes.

The art of letting go is often easier said than done but it is a skill that will be very beneficial in your business life. Accept the fact that we all get it wrong from time to time but learn your lesson and move on. The University of Life is offering PhDs daily for just about every small business I know.

What can you do today?

Are you hanging on to a business mistake that you made? Well, today is the day to let it go. It's time to move forward.

#100 Even better, learn from your competitors' mistakes

In the last tip we discussed the importance of learning from your business mistakes and moving on. An even better option is to be a close observer of your competitors and learn from their mistakes.

We tend to take a keen interest in what our competitors are doing and if you don't you should. Being aware of what is happening within your own market needs to be an accepted part of your business. As you observe your competitors see what they do well and what they do poorly. Clearly both bits of information provide you with an opportunity.

If your competitor makes an obvious mistake—perhaps they have changed their pricing structure and they have out priced themselves, or perhaps their latest advertising is ineffectual or their overall level of customer service has dropped—and you find out about it, their mistake can help your business to grow. This is especially so if you take the time to really think about where they went wrong and what was the main cause of their mistake—did they misread their customers, was there a change of staff or a change of owners or some other key contributing factor.

Being a successful entrepreneur involves being a good observer of the many different things that you can learn from or that can have an impact on your business. Learning from your competitors' mistakes is one way to avoid making them yourself.

What can you do today?

Think about your main competitor. What have they done well in the past few months and what have they done poorly? What lesson can you learn from what they did poorly? Start reviewing your competitors' mistakes and look for ways to ensure that you don't make the same ones.

#101 Don't become obsessed with your competitors

This is an interesting point and one that I have touched on elsewhere in this book: avoid the temptation to become obsessed with your competitors. I have encountered a lot of business owners whose entire life is based on what their competitors are doing. Every decision they make is the direct result of something the competition has done or is planning to do.

By all means have a healthy awareness of your competitors—I think this is essential to be truly successful in business, see tip 100—but don't build your business around what they are doing. Rather, focus on what you can do to lead the way.

Often this obsession is the result of insecurity and fear and as a result the reactive steps taken by the business reflect these negative traits. This is how price wars start—and no one wins a price war except the customer—advertising becomes ad hoc and knee jerk instead of systematic and well planned, and customer service is forgotten about as the business owner is too busy looking at what the competition is doing rather than what is happening within their own business.

Be aware of what your competitors are doing and evaluate their actions, but don't make their businesses the centre of your universe.

What can you do today?

Ask those people closest to you if they think you are obsessed with your competitors—they will know. Remember, though, if you are going to ask for their opinion, be prepared for the answer. If you get hostile because of the response maybe this reinforces the fact that it is time to let go.

Action pages

Things I need to do to make my business more successful.
91 Believe you are the best and you will become the best
Action required right now

....
....
....
....

Completed (date, time and by whom)

....
....

92 Enter your business in awards whenever possible
Action required right now

....
....
....
....

Completed (date, time and by whom)

....
....

93 Get your name in print—there are plenty of opportunities
Action required right now

....
....
....
....
....

Completed (date, time and by whom)

....
....

94 Be prepared to get up in front of a crowd—challenge yourself
Action required right now

....
....
....
....

Completed (date, time and by whom)

....
....

95 Being a green business is good for business
Action required right now

....
....
....
....

Completed (date, time and by whom)

....
....

96 Be supportive of competitors—even if it is one-sided
Action required right now

....
....
....
....

Completed (date, time and by whom)

. . . .

. . . .

97 Spend time researching your industry online
Action required right now

. . . .

. . . .

. . . .

. . . .

Completed (date, time and by whom)

. . . .

. . . .

98 Allow plenty of time to think—and less time to do
Action required right now

. . . .

. . . .

. . . .

. . . .

Completed (date, time and by whom)

. . . .

. . . .

99 Learn from your mistakes
Action required right now

. . . .

. . . .

. . . .

. . . .

. . . .

Completed (date, time and by whom)

....
....

100 Even better, learn from your competitors' mistakes
Action required right now

....
....
....
....

Completed (date, time and by whom)

....
....

101 Don't become obsessed with your competitors
Action required right now

....
....
....
....

Completed (date, time and by whom)

....
....

Brainstorming pages

Use these pages to write notes, comments, ideas or things to do regarding the preceding section. The aim is to improve your business a little every day, to make it more successful and for you to enjoy being an entrepreneur.

....

....

....

....

....

....

....

....

....

....

....

....

....

....

....

....

....

....

....

....

'You are the average of the five people you spend the most time with.'

Jim Rohn, self-made millionaire and successful author

Bonus section: 20 more tips to help build a winning business

As a diehard marketing man I can't help but feel the need to add value to everything I do. In this instance, the value add is this bonus section. Most of the tips and recommendations here are based on observations of winning businesses doing what they do best. Use the information accordingly and apply it to your own business.

102 Be one hundred per cent clear about what it costs to run your business
103 Without cash you are doomed
104 Don't stop marketing when business is good
105 Is money slipping through the cracks?
106 Embrace delegation
107 Stay focused—the more successful you become the more distractions will appear
108 Don't be afraid to tell people you are good at what you do
109 Find a mentor—but make it a good one
110 Learn to let go—if it doesn't work move on
111 Get the best professional advice possible
112 Expansion is great but can you afford it?
113 The simplicity of checklists

114 Be passionate about your business but learn the art of detachment
115 Run your business—don't let it run you
116 Never be afraid to put a proposal to someone
117 You don't have to work like a dog to be a success
118 Start an inspirational scrapbook and ideas box
119 A simple strategy to overcome the dreaded 'failure to implement'
120 If times are tough talk to someone about it—you will feel much better
121 Enjoy the journey—it will be a roller-coaster ride!

#102 Be one hundred per cent clear about what it costs to run your business

Do you know exactly (and I do mean exactly) how much it costs to run your business? If you don't, relax—most business owners don't. Most have a rough idea but not an exact amount. Well I can personally attest that this is one area of any business that needs to be looked at long and hard. If you don't know how much it costs you to open the doors every month you can never really know how much money you need to bring in to cover costs. And if you don't know this, you can get yourself into some serious trouble.

I ran a business for twelve months and I worked out it cost $20000 every month to operate. For some reason I never seemed to be getting ahead—there was never enough money to cover the bills. After twelve months I sat down and figured out where I was going wrong. I recalculated all of my monthly expenses, particularly the oddball amounts that are not as memorable as perhaps the rent or wages, and to my shock and horror I realised I was $10000 per month short in my previous calculation. It was actually costing me $30000 to run my business every month and I was just making enough to cover the $20000 figure I had in my head—not enough to cover costs in reality. If I hadn't picked this up it was only a matter of time before I went broke.

Now I ask just about all of my clients if they know what it costs them to run their business and very few can accurately answer the question. They often state that there are too many variables to know until after the month has passed but any accountant will be able to advise you how to allow for the variables. Even more importantly, always overestimate costs rather than underestimate. This way, you can be pleasantly surprised when the bills come in rather than terrifyingly shocked.

Figure out the exact cost of doing business on a monthly basis and you can then work out what it costs to run the business every week, every day and every hour. It is often a little scary to do this but it is also very liberating as it will give you a firm handle on exactly how much money you need to make to survive.

What can you do today?

Work out exactly how much it costs you to open the doors of your business every month. If there are figures you have to estimate, go on historical data and overestimate expenses rather than underestimate. Once you know this figure, make sure you monitor it against your income every month. It is a simple way of knowing where you are at.

#103 Without cash you are doomed

No business can operate without money hitting the bank account in a timely manner yet cash flow problems are still ranked number one as the biggest problem facing the vast majority of businesses. Sales are pretty good but getting the money in is the hard part.

If you are spending too much of your time juggling funds you have probably got a cash flow problem and this can be distracting for business. All of a sudden the vast majority of your energy is spent chasing money rather than making money.

You need to take control of your cash flow; perhaps it means being more careful and specific about your trading terms with clients. Perhaps it means having someone else control this side of the business so you can get on with making money. Perhaps your debts need to be restructured or reorganised or you may need an overdraft to smooth out the cash flow position. Whatever situation you are in, if you are constantly waiting to get paid and you can't pay bills, you need to do something about it.

Start with your accountant—they should be able to give you some good advice. You may need to hire the services of a credit controller whose main job is to make sure your money is flowing in rather than dribbling in, but you certainly need to address the situation.

Winning businesses need the undivided attention of the business owner and entrepreneur to grow and if their time is being used to chase debts the business will never be able to reach its full potential.

What can you do today?

If you struggle with cash flow do something about it. Call your accountant and ask for advice. If they can't help you, ask them to recommend someone who can. Talk to your business partners and mentors—ask them for advice on how they manage their cash flow and what they do when they are experiencing problems.

#104 Don't stop marketing when business is good

Many business owners stop marketing when their business gets busy. Then when their current workload eases they start marketing again. This stop–start approach to marketing is not ideal and it makes it much harder to build a business in a systematic and planned manner.

The best approach to marketing is to be consistent. Always have some marketing taking place even if you are already very busy. For some people this is a hard concept to put into practice. I use the momentum principle when it comes to marketing. Getting it going takes a lot of effort and it takes a while for the results to pay off. To keep it going doesn't take as much energy. If you have stop–start marketing you ultimately need to put more time, energy and money into it to get the results you need.

When planning your marketing you are not planning for today, you are planning for tomorrow. Personally I like to know I always have about ten proposals being considered by clients at any one time as this means my business's workload for the coming month will be on track with my forecasts. If I have more proposals pending I know I am in for a busy month and I can subcontract some extra help to accommodate this. If I have fewer than ten proposals I know I have to get out and look for more projects.

Take a long-term, more consistent approach to marketing your business and you will smooth out a lot of the peaks and troughs that cause all kinds of problems with cash flow and staffing. Your business workload will become more manageable and you will feel more in control of your business.

What can you do today?

Think about your marketing. Do you tend to stop–start market? If you do, start to think more long term about your marketing. The work you do today will get you customers tomorrow. A change in philosophy towards your marketing is the first step in the end of the stop–start marketing cycle.

#105 Is money slipping through the cracks?

I did an interesting exercise recently as part of an overall review of my business. On advice from one of my closest business mentors I set out to see if I could cut my business overheads by 20 per cent without affecting the way my business runs. That means I wanted the office to look smart and presentable, all the equipment to stay the same, the level of customer service to stay the same and the end quality of our products to be the same.

I explained to my team what I was trying to achieve and why I was trying to achieve it. I developed a range of financial incentives for every member of my staff so they had a personal interest in helping to cut the operating costs of the business and left it to them to come back to me with ideas. The results were impressive.

Within a few days they all delivered their ideas and suggestions. Most were excellent, some were not overly practical and some just would not work. We whittled down the recommendations and ended up with a specific list of ideas to achieve our objective. Then the staff were let loose to make the recommendations a reality.

The ideas included securing better prices on our purchasing by perhaps buying in bulk to get better rates, reviewing telecommunications expenses, utilising time better, implementing monitoring systems to keep track of expenses, adopting more detailed billing procedures to make sure all the costs were being charged appropriately and not slipping through the cracks, and getting rid of expenses that really had no bearing on the business but had simply evolved into an everyday expense. Now these may all seem logical but I was too busy processing work to take the time to review my operating expenses to come up with cost reductions.

The greatest cost saving came from reviewing my telephone and Internet expenses. We were spending approximately

257

$3000 per month. By changing my telephone carrier and renegotiating my Internet plan with my Internet service provider, the monthly bill dropped by $2000. Now that is an amazing saving, all done with a few telephone calls.

This process cut my monthly operating expenses from $30 000 to $23 000 per month. A huge change that added $84 000 to the annual bottom line. An impressive saving by any standard and all accomplished in a matter of days rather than months. Of course, the tough pill to swallow was that I had probably wasted hundreds of thousands of dollars in the previous few years by not paying enough attention to this end of the business, but never again. I repeat this exercise every six months, not with the intention of cutting costs by 20 per cent but just to make sure money is not slipping through the cracks because no one is paying attention to the details.

What can you do today?

Develop a cost-cutting plan that will not impact on the quality of your business, particularly the products or services you sell. If you have a team, get them involved, give them ownership and let them implement their own recommendations. The results will surprise and amaze you and your bottom line will love you.

#106 Embrace delegation

Most small businesses have key personnel. This is normally the owner or manager and they seem to be the person that receives a hundred phone calls a day, a pile of faxes, emails, letters and other forms of communication. If you are one of those people you will know and completely understand that at times it is extremely hard to move forward in your business because you get so bogged down in day-to-day activities.

This is an area I have often struggled with over the years. It is often easier to do things yourself rather than take the time to explain to a staff member how to do a particular job and then follow up to make sure it is done.

One of the most surprising observations I have made of successful business people is that often they are not actually that busy. Their day is full but they tend to start work and finish work at reasonable hours and they have a strong support team around them. They don't waste time doing small or repetitive jobs that waste their time. They expend their energy and personal resources on making decisions and moving the business forward.

A prime example of this is something as simple as using a courier. For years I would find myself driving all over town dropping off documents for clients. By the time I got myself organised, got in the car, found the premises, stopped and had a chat, did a few other chores and then headed back to the office I wasted at least one hour for every drop off I did. During a week I probably made ten to fifteen deliveries like this, so I was losing upwards of ten to fifteen hours per week in what I thought was an attempt to save a few dollars. When I sat down and worked out I was losing so much valuable time each week I quickly adopted the services of a courier who charges a few dollars for each delivery, saving me a lot of time when I can actually be making money.

I know this must seem obvious but at the time it wasn't to me. When I started my business I would only do one or two drop offs each week, so it really wasn't a big deal and to be honest it was nice to get out of the office. But over several years, business increased and before I knew it I was spending far more time doing a task that was basically sending me broke.

Delegation is a hard skill to learn and one that does not come naturally for many people. There are courses that can be done in virtually any city around the world and there are also some excellent books that cover the subject in detail. Some of my clients have found it particularly helpful to talk to friends and associates who are good at delegating to ask for tips and advice.

What can you do today?

Make a list of ten tasks you do every day that could be delegated to someone else to free up your time. If ten is too big a list, start with just one task that could be delegated to other members of your team (or outsourced).

#107 Stay focused—the more successful you become the more distractions will appear

This is a fact: as your business grows and you become more successful, more distractions will begin to appear around every corner. This is a dangerous time for any business and any easily distracted entrepreneur.

It is simple to argue that these distractions are wonderful opportunities coming your way and I am sure many of them are, but keeping a focus on your core business is essential. If you lose sight of this, by the time you regain your focus it may be too late.

I have witnessed this many times with growing businesses. The focus shifts from the business to the new opportunities and before long the main business starts to suffer. It is all about finding the balance between being open to new and exciting opportunities and still keeping an eye on your main business.

The hard part with this is that distractions are often more interesting and exciting. They often appeal to our egos. The wonderful thing about distractions and opportunities is they are not limited—if you miss one today, another one will come along tomorrow. Accepting this takes some of the urgency out of responding to every one that comes your way.

What can you do today?

When the next distraction (or opportunity) heads your way, stop and think about how it is affecting what you do. While contemplating this new possibility are there other parts of your business you will be neglecting? Being aware is halfway there to solving a potential problem—the other half is having the discipline to say no.

261

#108 Don't be afraid to tell people you are good at what you do

I often wonder why people are almost afraid to pronounce they are good at what they do but it is a real phenomenon. Sometimes I think it is because we don't always have a way of measuring or comparing what we do, so how can we know if we are good at what we do?

There are lots of ways to measure this; the most significant one is the amount of repeat business you get from your existing customers. If they keep coming back it is a pretty good sign that what you are doing is right. If your customers are telling their friends to use your business, likewise, it is a pretty good sign you are on the right track. If you are winning awards or industry recognition, again you are heading in the right direction. It is important to be proud of what you are doing and to tell your staff, your suppliers, the media, your friends and family, your colleagues and anyone else you can think of.

This doesn't mean you should stand on a street corner wearing a sandwich board saying, 'I am wonderful', but it does mean you should put letters of appreciation from customers in full view. If you win an award put the certificate or trophy in a place where everyone can see it. If your customers are happy, ask them to tell their friends.

I recently did a project for a company that owns a number of petrol stations. This company has a head office where staff and suppliers go but very few customers would ever visit. They have one huge wall covered in certificates and letters from customers, the awards that the business has won and the charities the business supports. While this is great, the business doesn't use any of these very significant promotional tools on their customers. I believe it is due to a sense of modesty but in the modern business world, modesty is a liability not an asset. Every petrol station this business owns should have copies of all of these letters and awards plastered in any available space. In fact they should make a brochure outlining what they do in the community and this should be given to every customer who visits the business. It reinforces they are not only good corporate citizens, but they are also good at what they do.

Be proud of your achievements and remember that people like to do business with people who are good at what they do.

What can you do today?

List five ways you can actively promote your business by telling your customers you are good at what you do and action them.

#109 Find a mentor—but make it a good one

Having a business mentor is a great idea and most successful entrepreneurs either have indirect mentors (people they model their own business philosophy and ambitions upon) or a direct mentor who helps them through their day-to-day decision making. If you have a personal mentor they can be an excellent sounding board to help build your business and, most importantly, your business skills.

I have had some wonderful mentors over the years—some older than me, some younger; men, women; qualified and unqualified. Most people will gladly give their time and wisdom to anyone who is keen enough to want to learn. That is the positive side of entrepreneurial pursuits—and anyone who is running their own business is definitely an entrepreneur.

My only word of warning here is to choose your mentors wisely. Not everyone is as squeaky clean as they should be and, remember, even the most respected individuals are human; they have all of the associated human strengths and weaknesses. Take your mentor's advice on board but make the final decision yourself.

What can you do today?

Is there someone you would like to have as your business mentor? Why not pick up the phone and give them a call? Respect the fact that everyone is busy and the person you call may not want the responsibility of mentoring you. But if you don't ask you won't know. If you are less comfortable contacting someone directly, think of the entrepreneurs you admire the most and buy their biographies (most will have them).

#110 Learn to let go—if it doesn't work move on

I have a close friend who would best be described as a serial entrepreneur, having succeeded at a host of business ventures including large-scale property developments, telecommunications, information technology, exporting and primary produce to mention just a few. He has led the way in so many business fields it almost defies belief, and he is incredibly modest and humble about his achievements. One of the greatest skills I learnt from him was the ability to let go of businesses that are no longer working.

This man has a host of joint venture partners, associated companies and general business associates around the world but he doesn't allow himself to get too attached to the deal he is working on. He will give any business 100 per cent commitment but as soon as the deal starts to fade, or business trends change and the writing is on the wall, he will quickly and unemotionally cut his losses and sell out his share or close the business accordingly in an ethical and responsible manner.

The ability to be detached from a situation and to be able to assess it for its true merits and potential is a skill that is often lost on business owners who will work themselves to death keeping afloat a business that has lost its way or lost its ability to work. Timing is everything in business (an old but accurate adage) and knowing when to let something go is not easy. Most people stay out of uncertainty of what to do next. This is often the reason people are resistant to change in general.

If a business situation or relationship is no longer working, be prepared to let it go and move on to your next challenge. Don't lament it—but learn from it. It is a time to get excited because your next opportunity is just over the horizon.

Likewise it may be prudent to lose some money now and walk away, rather than lose everything by hanging on. My belief about this is that if your business is really struggling and there is nothing in the near future that will cause a sudden and considerable change in fortune, think long and hard about continuing.

Over the years I have had a number of contracts that on the surface looked very prestigious and profitable. One in particular was managing the marketing of a large shopping centre. The monthly turnover that account provided was great but when I sat down and looked at the cost of managing it there was no money, just a lot of stress. So I made the decision to resign the account, much to the horror of my staff and the amazement of my competitors. In a few weeks I had replaced it with four new accounts that earned more than double the amount of income with far fewer company resources being committed as well as a lot less stress and grief.

What can you do today?

Are there any business situations, dealings or relationships that are holding you back from taking advantage of other opportunities? If so, today is the day to end them.

#111 Get the best professional advice possible

As I mentioned in the introduction to this book I am fortunate enough to spend a lot of time talking to many financially successful entrepreneurs in a multitude of different businesses from around the world on a regular basis. When I ask these people for their ideas and views on why one business is successful when another on a similar basis fails, a common reply is the use of professional advisers—lawyers, accountants, marketing and advertising consultants, human resource professionals, IT consultants and a host of others. The entrepreneurs know their individual knowledge is limited, after all you can know so much about business, and they need the right advice from the best sources possible. They go to experts and they use this information wisely.

Another interesting aspect to this is that they get this advice before they need it, so they have the time to consider their options and implement whatever actions are then necessary. They don't wait until the last minute to try and solve a problem.

I know I am generalising here, but it is a broad subject with a multitude of varying scenarios, however, I found this general openness to getting good advice a sound idea. Getting the best professional advice is a smart move and one that will pay for itself many times over. I wrote earlier about getting a professional to write your Business Plan, mainly because they can look at your business with fresh eyes. The same applies to just about any professional services provider; they can remove the emotional aspect of the business and offer an informed course of action based on the facts and current situation without the clouding of other issues that the business owner has to contend with.

I also read lots of newspapers and magazines and see the television shows that cover the demise of large corporations, often with the blame aimed at the professional advisers.

Personally I believe the vast majority of professional advisers are good at what they do. If you seek the best advice you can, you can then make any decisions that need to be made from an informed basis rather than from an emotive, uninformed position.

What can you do today?

Think about your business. Are there any specific areas where you need some really good advice but you have been putting off seeking it due to concerns of cost or not knowing who to talk to about it? Today is a good day to find a good professional adviser and start the process of solving the problem rather than ignoring it.

#112 Expansion is great but can you afford it?

Expansion is considered the natural route for most businesses to take. As the business grows and becomes more successful it attracts more customers, and it needs more staff to service the customers and larger premises to house the staff. But expansion can be a real trap if you haven't got the money behind you to fuel the expansion. You can easily get into financial trouble.

Expansion is an expensive exercise and it takes a lot of time, energy and focus from the day-to-day running of the core business. By all means expand but make sure you talk to your financial advisers and banker before you do—no matter how small your business is. Grow to a plan and control the expenditure so your long-term growth will be far more successful.

If you don't want to grow your business any larger that is fine. Resist the growth and focus on making the business the size you want it to be and make it magnificent. There is a lot to be said for a business that is controlled in size and run extremely well. Fine tune everything and get the formula right—someday you might want to expand and it is far easier to grow a successful, profitable, well-run business than it is to expand one that is just barely kept under control.

What can you do today?

Have you thought about what your plans are for expanding your business? Do you want it to stay the same size or do you want it to grow? If you want it to grow, how much do you want it to grow by? Today is the day to write your plan for expansion.

#113 The simplicity of checklists

Being organised is a significant step in the right direction when it comes to succeeding in business. Checklists are powerful tools to help get anyone focused. Personally I start every day with a checklist broken into three categories:

Work tasks that have to be done today
These are non-negotiable projects or responsibilities that really do need to be completed today. I like to knock them over early in the day just in case something unexpected comes up and throws my day into chaos.

Work tasks that I would like to get done today
These are the tasks I would like to get done today, but if I don't that is okay. Most importantly, if I don't get them finished I don't punish myself.

Things I am going to do today—for myself
The final part of my daily checklist includes several items that I want to do during the day, just for me. Generally this list includes fun things, maybe some exercise, lunch with a friend or spending some time on my own personal development.

Checklists can take many shapes and forms—you might like to make up a template on your computer or you might prefer using an exercise book so you can keep track of past lists. Finding your own technique is important. Many software applications offer quite sophisticated checklist or tasking options: again, they are relatively easy to use and they can be tied into an overall diary and calendar.

Finally, when it comes to checklists there are several tips to make them work more effectively. Don't put too many things on your list as you will never get them completed and always feel frustrated. Cross items off the list as you complete them (it feels great and gives you a sense of accomplishment). Finally, if you do other tasks during the course of the day put them on your list and cross them off again to give you a sense of achievement and accomplishment.

What can you do today?

Checklists are great tools for being more organised and for feeling like you are actually achieving results and getting tasks done rather than just treading water. Can you introduce checklists into your work to make your business successful? Can your staff use checklists to more effectively manage their work?

#114 Be passionate about your business but learn the art of detachment

Way, way back at the beginning of this book I wrote about the role that passion plays in building a winning business—and I sincerely believe it is the main ingredient. But while it is essential to be passionate about what you are doing it is also wise to learn the art of detachment.

In real estate we are always told, 'buy with your head not with your heart'. Don't get attached to property because you will pay too much. The same can be said for many business situations. There will always be another deal to be done, another customer or another opportunity. Be passionate enough to be enthused about the prospective outcome of the situation but patient enough to understand it is not the be-all and end-all. Some of my greatest business mentors have taught me this skill.

I struggled a lot at first because to me every opportunity that came along had to be the one. I soon learned that most opportunities are not as attractive underneath as they are on the surface and, even more interestingly, there was a never ending supply of them coming. Really, I am the one who can pick and choose my ventures. This is very empowering when you think about it.

The key with detachment is not to grow too fond of the outcome. For example, spending the money in your mind before you have the sale. This gives you a very significant attachment to outcome and if the deal doesn't come off you actually feel like you have lost something (which you never had in the first place).

This is a tough skill to master—but the benefits I have experienced are that I tend to make much better judgement calls, I do better deals and my passion is more focused.

What can you do today?

Learn to become detached from the outcome of a situation until the deal is done. Think about how you handle this situation at the moment. Do you count your chickens before they hatch—have you spent the money before the deal is done? The first place to start the change process is in your head.

#115 Run your business—don't let it run you

It's hard to build a winning business if you are not in control and many business owners will understand exactly what I mean by this statement. If your business is running you it's time to make some changes.

Many of the tips covered in this book address aspects of this concept but you need to make a very conscious decision that you are taking control of your business and it will be run on your terms. Feelings of being out of control, continually stressed out and over worked and fear of going broke all need to be released. Many of these will have built up over time and they will be so firmly entrenched that it is hard to get rid of them. It takes constant effort not to slip back into the old patterns and familiar ground.

Changing your business and taking control needs to be done one day at a time. It starts with small changes, a realisation that you will benefit from these changes and your enjoyment and satisfaction for your business will return.

This is not an easy tip to give tangible advice about. Personally, I know I feel much happier when I am in the driving seat of my business and it is developing and growing the way I want it to. The difference is all in the mindset. Change that and everything else will follow.

What can you do today?

Are you in control of your business or is it in control of you? To facilitate change you need to be ready for it and you need to be clear on how you want your 'new' business to look and feel. Write a few paragraphs on how you visualise your perfectly run business to be. What will your role be in this business? How much will you work and how much will you get paid? Visualising your business is the beginning of making it reality.

#116 Never be afraid to put a proposal to someone

Many enormously successful entrepreneurs have got to where they are with just one initial opportunity. This is the one that made them and started their career. Interestingly, these opportunities were generally created by the foresight of the aspiring entrepreneur and their ability to put a proposal forward, regardless of who the person receiving it was. They weren't daunted by the differences in the relationship—they had a good idea and they wanted someone to work with them to make it a reality.

I have discussed this with a number of entrepreneurs and they all agreed, they wouldn't hesitate to put a proposal to anyone, no matter who they are or how big the proposal may be. If money can be made, odds on someone will run with it, it's just a matter of finding the right person.

If you think you can solve a problem or help a business make more money (often the two are related) what have you got to lose by putting a proposal to them? Sure you face the risk of them doing it themselves, but you also face the opportunity of them being impressed enough with you to get you involved. There are ways you can protect yourself; confidentiality agreements are common in business but often they can be hard to enforce and the person you are submitting the proposal to may not want to sign it.

What can you do today?

The moral to this story is to think big and aim high. Put that proposal into place and it might be the big break you have been looking for.

#117 You don't have to work like a dog to be a success

There is nothing in the rule book that says to be successful at what you do you need to work yourself to death. Unfortunately, many business owners are so busy working that they are stopping themselves from being successful.

If you work too much you wear yourself out. You can't think clearly, you make bad decisions, you stop having fun, people close to you start to keep away, you start aging quickly and your health starts to suffer. It's hard to enjoy life if you are working 70 to 80 hours a week.

There is absolutely no advantage in working yourself this hard. In fact I go to great lengths to advise my clients to work less and have more holidays. There is never a good time or enough money—but you have to do it. To be a long-term success in your business you need a clear and focused mind and a healthy body. Neither of those can be achieved when you work like a dog.

I have been a workaholic for many years and it is only recently that I have managed to overcome this condition and life is much more enjoyable. I run my business a lot better and I make more money. It is a shame I worked so hard for so many years. Even though I have always enjoyed what I do I could have achieved the same results or probably better results by working less.

What can you do today?

If you are working like a dog, figure out how you can change the way you do things. First of all, stop saying how busy you are all the time. Change your talk and you change your thoughts. Make a list of what you can do today to reduce the amount you are working. If you work this hard for financial reasons, talk to your accountant or financial adviser to see if it is working—are you getting any closer to where you want to be? Maybe a fresh pair of eyes will point out a better way to do things.

#118 Start an inspirational scrapbook and ideas box

In my first book on marketing one of my recommendations was to start a marketing ideas box. The aim of this was to collect samples of good marketing that had caught my eye. It contained copies of brochures, advertisements from newspapers, promotional giveaways or anything that I felt was good marketing. The aim was to give me inspiration for when I was planning my own marketing. A quick rummage and I would find a good idea just waiting to be modified and used in my own business.

Well, I think that going one step further from this is also beneficial. In this case you can broaden the material you collect so it covers all aspects of running your business, not just the marketing. Cut out motivational stories from magazines, keep notes from any seminars you attend, letters from customers, photographs of your business (then and now) and anything else that evokes an emotion in you. This kind of inspirational box or scrapbook will be excellent for firing you up when you need it most. When you are feeling a little out of control or when things are starting to get on top of you, all of the items the box contains will have a message meant just for you.

How many times do you read an article in a newspaper and say to yourself that you should cut it out and keep it? What normally happens is it floats around your desk for a while and eventually you throw it out in a cleaning frenzy. What a waste. Now you can box it for later.

We all need a little inspiration from time to time, but even inspiration needs a little organisation to make it work. Make an inspirational box up and use it whenever you really need it.

What can you do today?

Start your own inspirational box today.

#119 A simple strategy to overcome the dreaded 'failure to implement'

FTI—failure to implement—is a nasty condition that can affect us all. It is when we have a pile of different things that need doing but we just can't seem to get around to doing them. There can be lots of reasons why we fail to implement them: they are unpleasant, you don't know where to start, you can't find the time or one of a hundred other possible reasons. Over time these FTIs can really start to get to you.

What really matters is overcoming the dreaded FTI and this is how I do it.

Firstly, I make up a list of any task I have failed to implement. When I first did that I had 20 items on the list. Under each one I wrote the specific reasons why I FTI this task and I was brutally honest—there was no need for vague excuses here, just the hard cold facts. Underneath my reasons I made a heading, 'What can I do right this minute to make this happen?'

I ended up with a concise list of the tasks that I failed to implement. Then I had my honest reasons for doing so and I had a specific action that I could take right now to remedy the situation. Within a day that list of tasks, which I just couldn't get around to, was completed and it felt great.

Now, whenever I am struggling to get particular tasks completed I repeat the same procedure and my FTIs rarely cause me any problems. This system works for me—hopefully it will work for you.

What can you do today?

If you have a list of FTIs, follow the procedure outlined above through to the end. You will be surprised how simply this eliminates the frustrations caused by not getting certain tasks completed.

#120 If times are tough talk to someone about it — you will feel much better

Business owners often wear a secret medal called the 'Stiff Upper Lip Medal'. It is awarded to those who take all of the negative things any business has to face and keep them inside, worried that if they tell someone about them, that they have had a tough week or that their business is financially tough, the person will think less of them.

I have found it to be quite the opposite. Most people are very understanding and the more experienced the person you confide in, the more understanding they will be. I don't think there are too many entrepreneurs who haven't had the odd sleepless night wondering how they were going to get through the mess they were in at the time. Things go wrong, businesses get into financial difficulties. It is a cycle and a business in trouble is just as normal as a business doing well. However, it sure is nice to be able to talk to someone when the going gets tough.

This is where a business mentor can help. If you don't feel comfortable talking to an associate see a professional. Maybe an accountant, maybe a counsellor, but whoever you see, once you can actually tell someone, 'I am worried that I might be going broke', it is a huge release. Then you can actually get on with the job of working to fix the problems rather than just worrying about them.

I read an excellent book on this subject a few years back called *How to Stop Worrying and Start Living* by Dale Carnegie, a man seriously ahead of his time. His advice was invaluable. It was based on some very practical and real situations, even though it was written over fifty years ago. The same pressures and risks apply today as they did back then. The best piece of advice I learned from this book was to imagine the very worst that could happen—and then accept it. So what does it mean if your business goes broke—sure you will have lost a lot of money, your ego will have been bruised and you will have gone through some pretty tough times, but no one can take away what you have learned. You might have to go and get a job and let someone else have the worry for a while. You could spend more time with your family and get your health and your life back on track. Maybe a few years down the line you can give it another crack, but it certainly isn't the end of everything. How many famous entrepreneurs have not gone broke at least once? Those that managed to avoid it have done so narrowly.

If your business is struggling or you are having a hard time dealing with business problems, talk to someone you can trust. Be open and honest and you will feel much better. If I have a friend in business who seems to want to have a chat and I can feel they are skipping around an issue but they can't bring themselves to broach the subject I will often make a statement like, 'What a week. I am having trouble getting money in and it's going to be a tough few months but I guess we all face times like this'. This often breaks the ice and lets them start off. It certainly is not difficult for me to do this because like any business, sometimes it's true.

What can you do today?

Who can you talk to if you are going through a tough time in your business? Is there someone who you think might be going through a difficult time who could use your help? Remember, if you are helping someone, what they tell you has to be locked in the vault, never to be passed on to anyone else.

#121 Enjoy the journey—it will be a roller-coaster ride!

Being an entrepreneur is a roller-coaster ride—all business owners face the same ups and downs, the same challenges, the same trials and tribulations and it's easy to get caught on the ride. The sad part can be that we get so caught up with the ride that we forget to take the time to enjoy it.

Running your own business has a huge amount of joy to offer. This can come from doing what you do really well, having happy customers, building a successful and impressive business, learning new skills and building a good team of people around you. Unfortunately these get lost in among paying the rent, a customer complaint, a supplier messing up an order, sick staff members, increasing competition and a host of other equally distracting day-to-day demands for your attention.

I recommend you take a few minutes each week and write in your diary or on a computer log of some sort what your achievements have been for this week. Just the good stuff—and the list can be as big or as small as you want it to be. It's best not to just focus on financial achievements, although these are without doubt important. It is interesting how doing this exercise balances your feelings towards how the last week has actually gone.

Good things don't often require any further action or follow up—they just happen and you move on. But the more trying details require your attention and focus, quickly over-shadowing the good that has happened. When you keep a log of the good things they become more concrete. I make a point of emailing everyone in my office whenever something good happens—maybe it is a nice call from a happy customer, an article in the paper about one of our clients, a new contract, something positive regarding a member of staff, sales figures and results this month or this year compared to the same time last month or year and so on. My staff all comment on how nice it is to hear these snippets of positive information coming from the boss.

Whichever way you want to do it is up to you. But take the time to enjoy the journey by reinforcing the positive things that happen during your working week.

What can you do today?

Think about the last week and make a list of all the good things that happened. It can be a little hard to remember them at first, but with a little training and routine you will start to form this list quite easily on a regular basis. Pass the information on to those around you.

Action pages

Things I need to do to make my business more successful.
102 Be one hundred per cent clear about what it costs to run
your business
Action required right now

. . . .

. . . .

. . . .

. . . .

Completed (date, time and by whom)

. . . .

. . . .

103 Without cash you are doomed
Action required right now

. . . .

. . . .

. . . .

. . . .

Completed (date, time and by whom)

. . . .

. . . .

104 Don't stop marketing when business is good
Action required right now

. . . .

. . . .

. . . .

. . . .

. . . .

Completed (date, time and by whom)

....

....

105 Is money slipping through the cracks?
Action required right now

....

....

....

....

Completed (date, time and by whom)

....

....

106 Embrace delegation
Action required right now

....

....

....

....

Completed (date, time and by whom)

....

....

107 Stay focused—the more successful you become the
more distractions will appear
Action required right now

....

....

....

....

Completed (date, time and by whom)

....

....

108 Don't be afraid to tell people you are good at what you do
Action required right now

....

....

....

....

Completed (date, time and by whom)

....

....

109 Find a mentor—but make it a good one
Action required right now

....

....

....

....

Completed (date, time and by whom)

....

....

110 Learn to let go—if it doesn't work move on
Action required right now

....

....

....

....

....

Completed (date, time and by whom)

....

....

111 Get the best professional advice possible
Action required right now

....

....

....

....

Completed (date, time and by whom)

....

....

112 Expansion is great but can you afford it?
Action required right now

....

....

....

....

Completed (date, time and by whom)

....

....

113 The simplicity of checklists
Action required right now

....

....

....

....

....

Completed (date, time and by whom)

....

....

 # 114 Be passionate about your business but learn the art of detachment
Action required right now

....

....

....

....

Completed (date, time and by whom)

....

....

 # 115 Run your business—don't let it run you
Action required right now

....

....

....

....

Completed (date, time and by whom)

....

....

 # 116 Never be afraid to put a proposal to someone
Action required right now

....

....

....

....

....

Completed (date, time and by whom)

....
....

117 You don't have to work like a dog to be a success
Action required right now

....
....
....
....

Completed (date, time and by whom)

....
....

118 Start an inspirational scrapbook and ideas box
Action required right now

....
....
....
....

Completed (date, time and by whom)

....
....

119 A simple strategy to overcome the dreaded 'failure to implement'
Action required right now

....
....
....
....

Completed (date, time and by whom)

. . . .

. . . .

120 If times are tough talk to someone about it—you will
feel much better
Action required right now

. . . .

. . . .

. . . .

. . . .

Completed (date, time and by whom)

. . . .

. . . .

121 Enjoy the journey—it will be a roller-coaster ride!
Action required right now

. . . .

. . . .

. . . .

. . . .

Completed (date, time and by whom)

. . . .

. . . .

Brainstorming page

Use this page to write notes, comments, ideas or things to do regarding the preceding section. The aim is to improve your business a little every day, to make it more successful and for you to enjoy being an entrepreneur.

....

....

....

....

....

....

....

....

....

....

....

....

....

....

....

....

....

....

....

....

....

....

....

Where to from here?

If you have got to this page and done everything in *101 Secrets to Building a Winning Business* I am absolutely certain that you will have an impressive business that is way out in front of your competition. But if you have got to this page and you are feeling a little daunted about where to start my advice is simple: break the process into small steps. It's like climbing a mountain. If I popped out today and tried to climb Mt Everest I seriously doubt I would get very far. But if I broke the whole process into small manageable chunks that I actioned over time, I believe I could get there.

So, grab a bookmark and find the one section that really struck a chord with you. This is probably the area where your business needs the most attention. Choose the point and address the issue it raised. Read the 'What can you do today?' tip and do it. Just the one. Tomorrow do the same process but move on to the next tip that caught your attention and implement it. Trying to address everything at once is just too big and too awesome a task for most people but if you break it into manageable chunks you will have a far greater chance of making headway.

I liken this to people going on a health binge, the infamous New Year's Resolution—on 1 January they are going to stop smoking, drinking, eating rich food, not exercising, working too hard . . . the list goes on. How can anyone live up to this enormous amount of change and expectation? But if they tried to do just one thing on their list, their chances of success would be greatly increased.

So make your 'business resolutions' realistic and work to a level that is good for you. It is far better to make even one change to your business rather than none at all.

'If you think you can do a thing or think you can't do a thing, you're right.'

Henry Ford

About the author

Andrew Griffiths is an entrepreneur with a passion for small business. From humble beginnings as an orphan growing up in Western Australia, Andrew has owned and operated a number of successful small businesses, with his first enterprise—at age seven—being a paper round. Since then, he has sold encyclopaedias door to door, travelled the world as an international sales manager, worked in the Great Sandy Desert for a gold exploration company and been a commercial diver. Clearly this unusual combination of experiences has made him the remarkable man he is.

Inspired by his constant desire to see others reach their goals, Andrew has written seven hugely successful books, with many more on the way. His *101 Ways* series offers small business owners practical, passionate and achievable advice. The series is sold in over 40 countries worldwide.

Known for his ability to entertain, inspire and deliver key messages, Andrew is also a powerful keynote presenter, who brings flamboyant energy and verve to the corporate world. All of this occurs from his chosen home of Cairns, North Queensland, Great Barrier Reef, Australia.

To find out more about Andrew Griffiths please visit the following websites:

www.andrewgriffiths.com.au
www.allenandunwin.com

Recommended reading

Canfield, J., *The Success Principles*, HarperCollins, London, 2005

Carnegie, D., *How to Win Friends and Influence People*, Simon & Schuster, 1936

— *Stop Worrying and Start Living*, Simon & Schuster, 1944

Gerber, M., *The E Myth Revisited*, HarperCollins, New York, 1995

Godin, S., *Purple Cow*, Penguin, New York, 2002

— *Small is the New Big*, Penguin, New York, 2006

Griffiths, A., *101 Ways to Market Your Business*, Allen & Unwin, Sydney, 2000

— *101 Survival Tips for Your Business*, Allen & Unwin, Sydney, 2002

— *101 Ways to Really Satisfy Your Customers*, Allen & Unwin, Sydney, 2002

— *101 Ways to Advertise Your Business*, Allen & Unwin, Sydney, 2004

— *101 Ways to Boost Your Business*, Allen & Unwin, Sydney, 2006

— *101 Ways to Have a Business and a Life*, Allen & Unwin, Sydney, 2007

— *101 Ways to Build a Successful Network Marketing Business*, Allen & Unwin, Sydney, 2008

Herald, J., *Get Motivated*, Allen & Unwin, Sydney, 2007

Lundin, S. and Paul, H., *Fish Tales*, Hyperion, New York, 2002

McGrath, J., *You Inc.*, HarperCollins, Sydney, 2003

O'Toole, T., *Breadwinner—A Fresh Approach to Rising to the Top*, Information Australia, Melbourne, 2000

Sharma, R., *The Greatness Guide*, HarperCollins, London, 2006

Switzer, P., *350 Ways to Grow Your Small Business*, Harper-Collins, Sydney, 2002

Recommended websites

www.andrewgriffithsblog.com.au
www.flyingsolo.com.au
www.jackcanfield.com
www.smallbusines.com
www.smallbusiness.co.uk

101 WAYS TO MARKET YOUR BUSINESS

Stand out from the crowd.

Here are 101 practical marketing suggestions to help you achieve dramatic improvements in your business without investing a lot of time and money.

Simple, affordable and quick, these innovative tips are easy to implement and will bring you fast results. Choose and apply at least one new idea each week or use this book as a source of inspiration for new ways to market your services, your products and your business itself.

With tips that take just a few moments to read, *101 Ways to Market Your Business* will help you find new customers, increase the loyalty of the customers you already have, create great promotional material and make your business stand out from the crowd.

INCLUDES 20 BONUS SUGGESTIONS TO HELP YOU ATTRACT NEW CUSTOMERS AND KEEP YOUR EXISTING ONES

101 WAYS TO ADVERTISE YOUR BUSINESS

Read this before you spend another cent on advertising.

Here are 101 proven tips to increase the effectiveness of your advertising. Use these tips to understand what makes one ad work while another fails and you will save a small fortune in wasted advertising.

With tips that take just a few moments to read, *101 Ways to Advertise Your Business* offers step-by-step advice on how to make an advertisement, how to buy advertising space and how to ensure that your advertisement is working to its full potential. Follow the tips and your business will soon be reaping the benefits.

INCLUDES A SPECIAL BONUS SECTION CONTAINING HUNDREDS OF THE BEST ADVERTISING WORDS AND PHRASES

101 WAYS TO REALLY SATISFY YOUR CUSTOMERS

Simple ways to keep your customers coming back.

Here are 101 practical tips for delivering service that exceeds your customers' expectations and keeps them coming back. In a world where consumers are far more informed, discerning and demanding than ever before, customer service is one of the main areas where a business can outshine its competitors.

Use these simple tips to improve your customer service and you will be well on the way to success and profitability. With tips that take just a few moments to read, *101 Ways to Really Satisfy Your Customers* teaches you to identify what customers expect, and details simple suggestions that will enable your business to exceed these expectations and reap the rewards.

INCLUDES 20 BONUS TIPS THAT WILL REALLY IMPRESS YOUR CUSTOMERS

101 WAYS TO BOOST YOUR BUSINESS

Energise your business today!

Here are 101 powerful tips to kick-start your business and unlock some of the potential that may be struggling to break through.

With tips that take just a few moments to read, *101 Ways to Boost Your Business* shows you how to make your business better and ultimately more profitable. These no-nonsense tips can be actioned immediately, so you will see results quickly.

These tips cover a host of everyday business issues, and are equally applicable to all industries in each and every corner of the world. They will save you thousands of dollars.

INCLUDES 20 BONUS TIPS THAT WILL RECHARGE YOUR BUSINESS

101 WAYS TO HAVE A BUSINESS AND A LIFE

Put the passion back into your business and your life

Is your business all-consuming? Are you tired of feeling over-whelmed every day? Would you like to take control of your life again?

If, like most business owners, you are struggling to balance your business and your life, don't worry! *101 Ways to Have a Business and a Life* provides simple, practical ideas that will help you to identify the reasons behind this lack of balance and what to do about it. Andrew Griffiths has consulted thousands of business owners around the world and compiled their experiences and coping mechanisms into one easy reference book. All of the tips can be implemented quickly and at little or no cost. You can be the boss of your business and your life.

INCLUDES 20 BONUS SUGGESTIONS TO ENSURE THAT YOU'RE THE ONE CALLING THE SHOTS IN YOUR BUSINESS WORLD

THE *101 WAYS* SERIES

101 WAYS TO BUILD A SUCCESSFUL NETWORK MARKETING BUSINESS

The concept of network marketing is sound: build relationships with like-minded people and sell quality products and services within this network. Some people make amazingly high incomes from their network marketing businesses, but others fall by the wayside. Why do some fail while many prosper?

101 Ways to Build a Successful Network Marketing Business gives smart, practical tips on how to succeed at network marketing. It explains simple and commonsense ways to treat any network marketing business like a mainstream business. By taking away the mystery, it shows you how to turn every venture into a success.